The Fabulous Baker Brothers

Tom & Henry
HERBERT

headline

To Mrs Herbert and Mrs Herbert

Some of the content in this book has previously been published in Fork Magazine –
www.forkmagazine.com. Their permission to reprint this material has been granted
and Tom and Henry would like to thank them for their continued support.

First published in 2012
by HEADLINE PUBLISHING GROUP

1

Cataloguing in Publication Data is available from the British Library

978 0 7553 6365 0

Project Editor: Mari Roberts
Recipe Tester: Signe Johansen
Designed by Smith & Gilmour, London
Illustration by Johanna Kindvall
Fabulous Baker Brothers logo by Brad Evans

Printed and bound in Great Britain by Butler Tanner & Dennis

Headline's policy is to use papers that are natural, renewable and recyclable products and
made from wood grown in sustainable forests. The logging and manufacturing processes
are expected to conform to the environmental regulations of the country of origin.

HEADLINE PUBLISHING GROUP
An Hachette UK Company
338 Euston Road
London NW1 3BH

www.headline.co.uk
www.hachette.co.uk

This book is published to accompany the television series The Fabulous Baker Brothers produced by betty for Channel 4.

CONTENTS

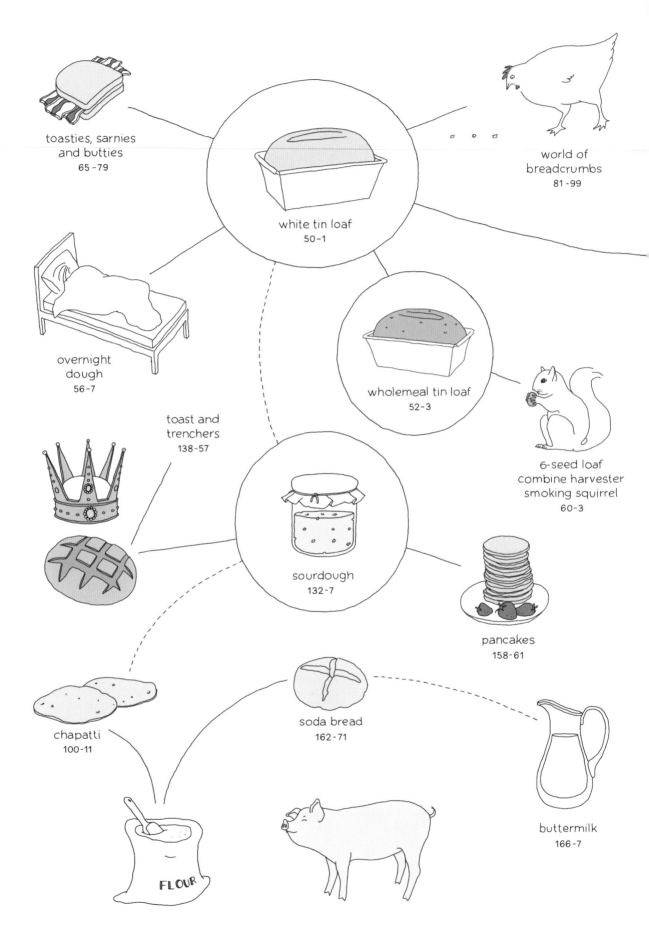

FLOUR

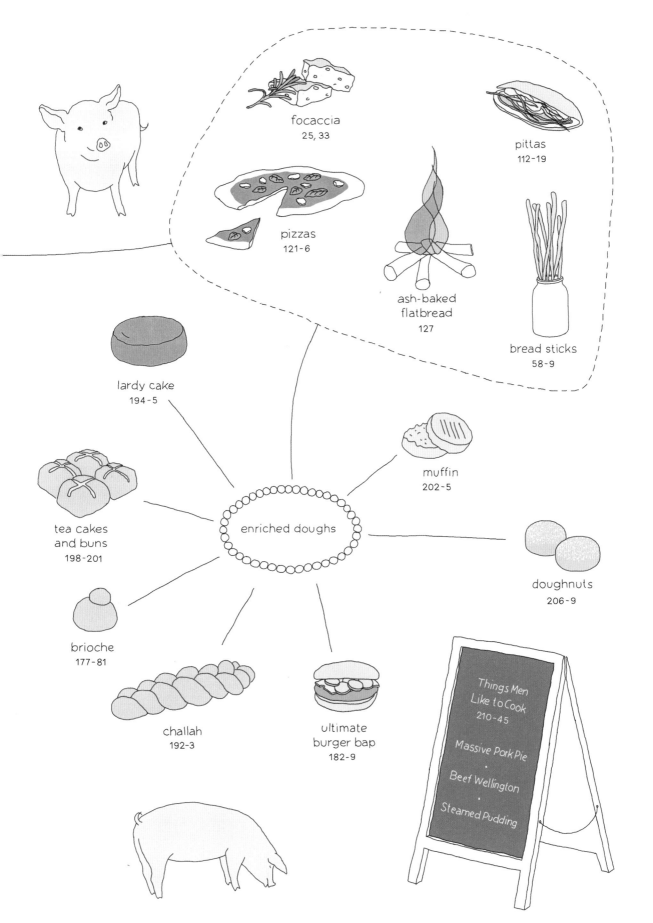

focaccia
25, 33

pittas
112-19

pizzas
121-6

ash-baked
flatbread
127

bread sticks
58-9

lardy cake
194-5

muffin
202-5

tea cakes
and buns
198-201

enriched doughs

doughnuts
206-9

brioche
177-81

challah
192-3

ultimate
burger bap
182-9

Things Men
Like to Cook
210-45

Massive Pork Pie
·
Beef Wellington
·
Steamed Pudding

AN INTRODUCTION TO
HOBBS HOUSE

BREAD: THE BEGINNINGS OF EVERYTHING. AND ONE THING LEADS TO ANOTHER…

The bread is in the middle of the table. People rip into it and conversation flows around it. It's great if the bread can get a nod or a bit of appreciation, but that's not why you make it yourself. You make it yourself because it's rewarding, because of the way it fills your home with the smell of warm fresh baking, and because you're *making something*, which is great if you've been sitting in front of a computer all week. And you're prototyping all the time, so if it goes wrong one time, what's the worst that can happen? It might be burnt, but you can scrape it off, or it might be stodgy in the middle, but you can cut out the middle and throw it away, and no one is going to die – unless you set fire to the kitchen. Once you've got the basics, you can play with it. There are limitless options.

We want to breathe a bit of joy into breadmaking, and debunk the myths and make it accessible and fun.

Henry: 'It's just mixing stuff.'

Tom: 'We want to take the fear out.'

Henry: 'It's child's play.'

Tom: 'My two oldest kids – they're ten and eight – have got their own jars of sourdough and they love baking. I don't ask them to do it. They get

Grandpa to compare their loaves, which he has to be very diplomatic about.'

We want to show how once you've mastered this, you can do this and this. Our ethos is not: here's a recipe for one thing we like, here's another – it's about how all the dishes connect together, with a natural progression from one thing to the next. Once you've made one sort of bread, you can easily make another, then another, then you can make really great meals around it. And we see this book as a way of sharing that with thousands of people.

Let's start with flour and water. At its most basic, that's all you need. To make chapattis, for example, you need some flour and water and a flame. Maybe not the most beautiful bread in the world, but mighty fine with curry.

Henry: 'I've often made a chapatti in five minutes and eaten it then and there. OK, they are better rested, but it's just flour and water, mixed together, cooked in a dry pan over heat. They puff up like a pitta, then you put them on a naked flame, using tongs, and they kind of burn in spots – and then you just eat them.'

Our next step in breadmaking is sourdough, a risen bread, consisting of flour and water, raised with a flour-and-water sourdough culture, and seasoned with sea salt. Sourdough is an ancient way of rising bread that has great flavour. The culture itself isn't necessarily dough-like, it's more of a paste, a blend of flour and water that's left to ferment and develop its own wild yeasts. A by-product of the fermentation process is carbon dioxide, and if you make a stretchy dough, the carbon dioxide catches in it – creates little bubbles – and leavens your bread. We can make beautiful bread just around that basic idea. Then there are variations – you can use wholemeal flour, which is denser than white and has a more nutty flavour; or you can use spelt (an ancient wheat), or rye. You can add other ingredients – seeds, nuts, fruit, cheese. And if you're making sourdough bread, then you're keeping and feeding your sourdough culture, and that means you can make sourdough pancakes, which everyone loves.

There's something of a myth that if you don't feed a sourdough culture, it will die. This isn't true. At home we keep the sourdough in the fridge and we take it out and feed it when we need to get it going. If you do it that way, your sourdough will outlive you.

Henry: 'I found a sourdough mix in the back of the fridge, been there five months, and three days later it's bubbling again.'

Tom: 'The sourdough we use in the bakery is over fifty years old. It had our grandfather's hands in it.'

The next step is the yeasted loaf, a white tin loaf – a good recipe that works, keeps well and tastes good. A small change of ingredient or method and the basic white loaf can be made into, say, pitta bread, or lush, thin pizza bases, or crunchy-bottomed focaccia. Then you can enrich it by swapping the water with milk or buttermilk or adding eggs, and you can make challah or even our ultimate burger baps. Following the trajectory of sweetening and enriching will take you to the jewel in the crown: a beautiful brioche.

Tom: 'What I'm saying is that once you've nailed one basic loaf, then you're really close to another loaf entirely.'

Then there are soda breads: bread raised with bicarbonate, cooked on a tray, with a cross cut into the dough. Our starting point is a spelt wholemeal because that's easier to digest, but of course you could use regular wholemeal. Soda bread is quick to make and tasty. Once you've got the basics, you can tweak it. We have a soda bread packed full of seeds that's made in a tin, and a recipe for white soda bread with honey in it and some fruit.

Then, of course, you can continue along the trajectory and go off into Pie World, adding fat to flour and changing the fat–flour–liquid ratios to make pastries, pancakes, Yorkshires, cakes, biscuits . . . Cupcakes aren't our bag. This is a man's cookery book. But that doesn't mean that, as a guy, you shouldn't know how to make something chocolatey.

Henry: 'You know, chocolate cake was very useful when I was courting my wife. And I still make it for her, when she wants to be cheered up.'

Tom: 'Making the Christmas cake is a manly thing to do. It's heavy, it's boozy, it's blokeish. Then we've got lardy cake, that's a kind of bread,

Ro Richards teaches Tom how to make lardy cake

but it's also a heritage recipe, it comes from the West Country. Ro, a 94-year-old baker, showed me how to make it. He hadn't made lardies for thirty years; he had the recipe written down, but success was nothing to do with the recipe, it was all in the method. They're phenomenal. A great recipe saved from extinction.'

Henry: 'They're crispy. It's kind of hot lard that's caramelised, and they're always massive—'

Tom: 'Don't eat more than one a day!'

Our own heritage recipe is the overnight loaf, the Sherston, which goes back to our great-grandfather, Thomas Herbert. Like many great ideas, this loaf was an answer to a problem. Yeast used to be very expensive, so bakers used the least amount of yeast they could and gave the dough plenty of rising time to compensate. The bread is still popular now, not because yeast is expensive any more, but because it's got a great flavour, and makes the best toast in the world. It's proper bread. The Sherston is our best-selling loaf at our family bakery, Hobbs House in Gloucestershire. It makes the older generation go all dewy-eyed and say, 'It tastes like bread used to taste,' and it makes the younger generation, who've been brought up on industrial bread, open their eyes to how great bread can be.

Tom: 'It was in researching for a programme I did called *In Search of the Perfect Loaf* that I came across my great-grandmother's birth certificate from 1887, where her father's occupation was listed as Baker. This was Mabel, she grew up and married Thomas Herbert, and he was a blacksmith in a village called Down Ampney in the Cotswolds, near us. Then one day the co-op that owned a lot of the land

Thomas and Mabel Herbert, the baker's daughter, Tom and Henry's great-grandparents

brought in their own farrier, and effectively put him out of business. He had six kids and there was no welfare, and his wife persuaded him to hang up his leather apron in exchange for a linen one, and convert the forge to a bread oven. And it was disastrous. The bread was really quite bad. They had a strong Christian faith, and they were on their knees praying for something to happen, when – the story goes – there was a trill on the bell and it was a local sundries man, who sold fat and yeast among other things, and he'd heard there was a new baker. He saw their plight and bailed them out, showing them what to do, and we've been baking ever since. That was 1920.'

This is where the overnight loaf comes in.

Henry: 'I think other bakers did it as well.'

Tom: 'Yes, the overnight dough wasn't our family's invention, it's what we adopted. Our recipe was from Mr Thompson, a baker in the local village of Sherston, who showed us how to do it. That's why we call the loaf the Sherston today; it roots it to that time and place, and honours a baking tradition. And it's still a great way of making wonderful bread.'

The story is that our great-grandfather would sleep on the dough bin and the rising dough would tip him off in the morning when it was time to work: long before cock crow.

Henry: 'He probably only did it after he'd had a tiff with Mabel.'

Tom: 'It's a heck of a way to wake

Herbert's bakery, 1955

up. That's the power of rising dough.'

Henry: 'It would definitely push you off.'

Tom: 'I've had the therapy for the bad dreams about being trapped in a room by rising dough, unable to escape…'

In time, Thomas's son David, our grandfather, went to Bristol, looking for work. He went into all the bakeries asking if they needed any staff, and they all said no. But the last one he walked into, after saying they weren't taking anyone on, announced that in fact they were planning to retire. They offered to sell Grandpa the bakery, and he said yes. So virtually the next day Grandpa was running his own shop. He developed something of a baking empire, with twenty-two hot bread shops at one stage.

Tom: 'As a family of bakers, we haven't just been in one place. We've got cousins who are bakers, and uncles. People come to us and say, "Oh, I'm sorry to tell you this, but the such and such bakery in Bristol, their bread is as good as yours," and I say, yes, well, that's my uncle. We're the non-violent baking mafia of the South West.'

In 1961, the Chorleywood industrial bread-manufacturing process came in. Food technicians and scientists discovered that you could make bread really fast on a large scale, often using lower-grade flour, which meant that bread could be made widely available at a low price. Of course, little regard was paid to things like quality, digestibility and flavour.

Trevor and Polly Herbert, the parents

Baby Tom, born into bread

And as the Chorleywood process took hold, bakers were encouraged to club together and have one big bakery and have the bread delivered in the morning for them to sell in their shops – and this, for a lot of people, was a dream. That's the path the industry went down, but we've never been part of that. Grandpa David stuck to his guns and kept making bread the traditional way. He was a bit of an outcast, a maverick, but he was just ploughing his own furrow. People have always wanted his bread. He ended up in Montpelier, the cosmopolitan, bohemian part of Bristol, and in the 1960s there were people from all over the world living there, and they wanted sourdough, and pitta bread, and focaccia, and other kinds of real bread. There was a market. And there was plenty of labour too. David Herbert was a firm believer that *anyone* could bake. He employed ex-cons fresh out of prison and taught them how to bake. While

for his father it had been yeast that was the most expensive part of the process, for him it was flour. He began by getting organic wheat from the Isle of Wight and milling it in the bakery, and then in time he ended up with a farm, where Mum and Dad still live, on the Cotswolds escarpment, where he grew and milled 600 acres of his own flour. We sold the mill to Shipton Mill, with whom we work very closely now.

Tom: 'Back in 1981, when I was very young and before Henry was born, my father and grandfather tried to get into the Guinness Book of Records for the fastest-ever loaf from field to table: an hour and a half. It was a great publicity stunt. Today, of course, we'd be trying to do the slowest! There's a film clip of it, some footage taken from a helicopter, and it's great, seeing my dad at my age, baking in a tie – wearing Sunday best because he was going to be on the telly. He took ten precious seconds to add

David Herbert going for the Guinness Record
for the world's fastest loaf, 1981

Trevor outside Herbert's Bakery, which has become
Hobbs House Bakery and Butchery, Chipping Sodbury

black treacle. I asked him why, and he said, 'So it tastes great.' I think that sums up a lot about how we bake. My brother George and I went up in the helicopter. So I grew up above a bakery kind of thinking this is what you do: bake bread, try for world records, go up in helicopters, have adverts in the local cinema. For me, as a lad, being a baker was exactly what I wanted, I never really wanted to do anything else. And it seemed a very gettable thing, even though Dad worked incredibly hard. When I was growing up he was always in this hot environment with banging tins and Bruce Springsteen and Roxy Music blaring out. By the time I got to about six, he'd let me double-jam the doughnuts, and recently we found

the jammer, the same old bit of kit, and it made me feel so nostalgic, that galvanised stainless-steel pump. There was always work, jamming, traying up stuff from the freezer, and then in time getting shown how to bake. The shop was our kitchen and living room – and it's where we still are, and where Henry has the butchery. What was our living room would fill up with bread and you'd have a queue of people and by the end of the day it would all be gone.'

People loved the bread, but the business could only grow as fast as we could train people to bake it. Labour became the most difficult part of the equation. The hours are antisocial, so it's not a given that people will stay. Only about half the people we trained

Tom, aged 13, and sister Clemmie, selling drop scones on a Victorian Evening

Henry, aged 13, baking in Tom's kitchen

stuck at it, so it's taken a long time to grow. But the ones who stayed, they became part of the family. There are people who've been with us for ever. We have apprentices working with us too, and recently one lad won Young Apprentice of the Year in the South West. The training is something we take very seriously. We want to train the next generation of craft bakers, and maintain the tradition of passing on methods and techniques.

Tom: 'Ten years ago I won Young Baker of the Year, after having done eight years of shift work, working nights, learning my craft. Winning that award showed me there was a whole world out there. I'd got into doing country markets, and baking my own

bread on a Sunday when we weren't open, and taking my dad's old bookshelf, which was a French bread rack, and displaying and selling my own bread for a bit of pocket money. In the 1980s Hobbs House built up a reputation for being in the vanguard of baking when we developed a range of olive breads, sun-dried tomato breads, pecorino and red onion, and so on. There was a great buzz about it and we won an award for the loaves. The trend caught on very widely. Then I, as the new generation, wanted to do my own thing. What interested me was the history of bread, and how you could bake the best possible simple, unadorned loaf. By the time I won Young Baker of the Year I already had some awards under my belt for my rye sourdough. It found a market and became one of our most successful loaves. I began by doing a breadmaking course for the Vegetarian Cookery School in Bath. That got me teaching, and I loved it, and soon I opened our place in Nailsworth: it's a café and open-plan bakery, and everything is centred around the oven and the baking courses. Ever since then we've been teaching, and baking, and my wife and I have had four kids, and I've constantly tried to find out a bit more about how to explain what I do to other people.'

Henry: 'I'm a lot younger than Tom. From the age of twelve I knew for certain that a life in food was the only way for me. I wake up hungry and my mind is on food for the rest of the day. I dream of doughnuts, carrots and beef. For my thirteenth birthday I was given a set of chef's knives. I worked in Tom's café in Nailsworth as a teenager, then I packed my bag and trotted off like Dick Whittington to London Town where I studied for my diploma while working in the kitchen of a fine pub, the Coach and Horses in Farringdon. At the age of twenty-one, I was given the chance to return to the pub as head chef, and with little idea of how much it would involve, but with a huge amount of energy and commitment, I jumped in.

At twenty-two I got to represent the South West on *The Great British Menu* on BBC2, which was a great honour. I didn't win, but as a chef only a year out of college I felt I'd done all right just to be on it. When the opportunity came up to take on the butcher's next to my family's bakery, I jumped at that too. I've always applied the principle that if you put everything into a job then it rewards you two-fold. Now I'm back home, running the Hobbs House Butchery with my team there.'

Tom: 'It's a great arrangement. Henry sends up the pie fillings, and we take a break from baking to make pastry, and together we turn out amazing pies. Or lardy cake: he's got the lard; I've got the flour. You know, I'm genetically modified for baking. I have exceptionally large palms, which is great for kneading, and magnificent eyebrows, which stops the sweat of a hot bakery getting into my eyes. And perhaps I'm not six foot four because I'd get backache all the time. Just give it another five generations, and because the most useful piece of equipment for baking bread is the dough scraper, we'll have flat edges to our hands.'

Peace and loaf,

Tom and Henry

THE
BAKER

THE JOY OF BREAD

Bread on the table is a sign that all is well, and to have the ability to make it yourself is one of life's top joys. It might take a few attempts, but once you've got the knack of making a basic bread dough, you've got the knack for life, and the bread gets better and better every time you make it. Your confidence soars, and your imagination can be let loose. You can do so many things with it. You've got people coming round, and you want to make something simple but great that's going to greet them with a fantastic aroma when they arrive at your door. How about a focaccia? You make a basic white dough up to the first rise, then you stretch it to fill the biggest roasting tin you've got, put tasty things on top – garlic, onions, rosemary, whatever – let it prove, then put it in a very hot oven for 15 minutes, timing it so that when your guests arrive they are going to get this amazing smell of freshly baking bread and aromatic toppings. What makes this extra fantastic is some olive oil in the bottom of the tin, three or four good glugs, and then baking it on a hot stone in the oven. It's like a savoury version of a doughnut, crunchy and warm and delicious. *That's how great baking is.* It's like when you scratch the belly of a dog and its leg goes on a mad shake, it's that kind of feeling – you know it's just right. In this chapter are all the fundamentals you need to know, starting from the very beginning, with flour, water, yeast and salt.

INGREDIENTS

Flour, water, yeast and salt. That's essentially it.

FLOUR

Ground-up edible stuff. There are many different kinds. Learn to sort the wheat from the chaff: find the flour that's right for you and, as soon as you know you're compatible, you can upgrade to a larger, more economical sack. As the main ingredient, the type and quality of the flour you use will be pivotal in determining the flavour and look of your bread. You can't make great bread with poor ingredients.

Most of the flours used in baking are from the wheat family, including spelt, and I often use rye. Many other cereals can be ground into flour, but wheat is the most common for bread because of its gluten-forming ability. This gives it the power, when mixed with water and given a good kneading, to s-t-r-e-t-c-h, and allows you to make a bread, pastry or bun that will hold together, puff up and rise. A wheat flour's gluten-forming potential is largely determined by its protein content. Flours with a high amount of protein are known as strong, or bread, flour. Strong flours with lots of elasticity potential are also used for pasta, and weaker flours are used for cakes or baked things that need to be short, in other words, soft, light, crumbly, melt in the mouth.

Milling can make a difference to quality. Traditional stone-grinding retains more of the goodness of the grain than modern steel-roller milling. Part of the pleasure of baking, for me, comes from the stories and traditions that surround it, and I find making a day trip to a water or wind mill is a great way to connect with this vital ingredient, learn of its provenance, and keep an ancient craft alive.

Flour, after milling, might be sieved. Wholemeal flour retains all of the grain, but white flour has the bran and other brown parts of the grain sieved out. This goes for spelt and rye too (light and dark rye). The bran part of wholemeal is hygroscopic – it continues to absorb water for quite a while after you have mixed it – so take care to work wetter to start with (if the recipe is for white dough, use about 10 per cent more water) and expect the dough to dry a little as it rests. Bran has no gluten-forming potential, so products made with wholemeal flours do not rise or stretch as much as white flours. But they do have a great flavour, and because of the higher fibre content, they are probably better for you too.

WATER

Typically, the wetter the dough the better. When you begin to knead, if you're doing it by hand rather than in a mixer with a dough hook, the dough is going to stick to your fingers and palms. Resist the temptation to add more flour, and bear with the stickiness until the dough has started to develop. A dough that feels loose and wet at the outset is much better than one that is tight and unyielding. I've given water quantities in the recipes that follow, but they are only guidelines. All flours have different water-absorbing abilities. As you get used to a flour, you'll get a feel for how much water it needs. If you do want to add flour to a very wet dough, do so only when you're sure you have to.

Tap water, aka sky juice, is fine. Of course, if you want to avoid the things that might be found in tap water, then knock yourself out and use spring water. But I always use tap. The more important thing to consider with water is its temperature. Tepid, or body temperature, is ideal: this is the level where yeast performs best. I gauge it by sticking my hand in the jug of water; if it feels neither hot nor cold, then it's about right. If you add cold water to a dough, it can slow it down. This might be useful. If your plans for the day mean you'd like to leave your dough hanging around a bit while you go off and do something else, you can slow the rising process down by adding cold water. Warmer water can speed the process up, but anything near boiling will kill the yeast.

YEAST

In the bakery, we've always used fresh yeast: *Saccharomyces cerevisiae* to give brewer's yeast (baker's yeast) its Latin name. It has a great flavour, it's easy to use, and I have an affinity for it. At home, however, I use dried yeast. You can get super-fast-acting yeasts, but they are to be avoided; this rocket fuel doesn't yield good results, just fast doughs that are out of kilter with the needs of home baking. Look for a dried yeast that is nothing more or less than yeast that has had the moisture taken out of it. It's a good idea to add the dried yeast back into water at the beginning of your recipe and give it a scram with a fork to make sure there are no lumps. Often the packet instructions suggest you leave the yeast in water for 15 minutes, but I find the time it takes to weigh out the rest of the dough is sufficient. If a recipe calls for fresh yeast and you only have dried, use half the amount: 10g of fresh becomes 5g of dried, and vice versa. If you've got fresh yeast, it'll keep for a couple of weeks in the fridge. If it becomes crumbly, it's starting to go over, so just weigh in a little extra. If it's becoming runny, it's starting to break down and it probably isn't worth using. Fresh yeast should be bouncy, with a window putty consistency. You can freeze fresh yeast, though I've never had much joy with it. If you live near a bakery and can get fresh yeast, that's great – but I have access to it in my bakery, yet I still use dried at home.

Recipes that don't require baker's yeast include flatbreads such as chapatti, and certain raised breads, such as soda bread, which uses bicarbonate of soda, and sourdough, which uses a flour-and-water fermentation. All these are delicious in their own right, and are also options for people with yeast intolerance. A slow-fermented loaf, like our overnight dough, which is made with much, much less fresh yeast than a commercial loaf and given a long, slow fermentation time, is also easier to digest. If you've had a diet of commercial bread and have been put off or advised against eating bread at all, you may find this makes all the difference.

SALT

Salt is used as a seasoning: wheat and other flours have great flavour, but unless they're seasoned, you don't get the full benefit. I prefer to use sea salt. It's more expensive, but it's pure and you tend to use less of it. At the bakery and at home I like to use sea salt from Cornwall and Wales, but it's a matter of individual preference. We're all advised to keep the salt in our diet to a minimum, so I'm in favour of seasoning your bread well and having unsalted butter on it. I think that's the right way round.

Salt also helps to control the fermentation: it slows the process down by inhibiting the yeast. If you leave the salt out of a dough, it will be much more flighty. Like a teenager on its first holiday to Newquay, it goes crazy. It bubbles up and ferments and doesn't develop the same flavour. It's best not to put the salt and yeast into direct contact but to add them either side of the flour.

ENRICHERS

Traditionally, lard, a plentiful and cheap product in this country, would have been added to some doughs, but this has fallen from favour. It's obviously not suitable for vegetarians, and has quite a strong taste. Some classic old recipes using lard, like lardy cake (see page 194), are just wonderful. Butter is rich, and beautiful in something like brioche (page 177).

Oils for baking are all about the flavour and the smoke point. I'm using more and more rapeseed oil. I love the flavour, and it grows locally; it's Britain's answer to olive oil. Olive oil is, of course, important for Mediterranean-type breads, such as focaccia. Curiously, crusty French rolls don't have any fat in them; you can make your dough crustier without fat. The quantity of oil to add to a dough is normally around 5 to 10 per cent of the flour weight.

Eggs enrich a dough (see challah, page 192, and doughnuts, page 206, for example). Sugar is used for sweetness and caramelisation. Sometimes sugar is added in small quantities for long-fermentation doughs, like the overnight dough (page 56). Yeast eats and lives off the sugars naturally found in flour, so if your dough is left too long to rise, it can eat all the sugars, leaving you with a dull-looking loaf. A tiny amount of sugar in an overnight dough can help avoid this, resulting in a golden crust.

Seeds, cheese, herbs, fruit, olives, chocolate: any manner of ingredients can be added to basic dough. As a rule, add in at 15 per cent of the flour weight. For spices and strong seasonings, use an amount closer to the salt weight.

TWEAKING

Both Henry and I strongly recommend you 'tweak' our recipes to suit yourself. If you find a dough is too salty, say, then put less in next time. You can tweak water up or down, and indeed you might have to, because, as I've explained, different flours absorb different quantities of water. This is why the experience of baking is all-important: the more you do it, the more you get a feel for it. Keeping a notebook in the kitchen and making notes as you go along is also a good idea, especially when you are starting out.

Focaccia, for example, is great tweaking territory. If you are Italian, or a purist, you might consider it appropriate only to have sea salt or rosemary on top, but being in Gloucestershire we've bastardised it, and when we're at home and we've got something in the back of the fridge that needs eating up, we'll make focaccia. It's a blank canvas. All you need is the dough after the first rising, loads of olive oil underneath, more olive oil and whatever else you fancy on top, a really hot oven (240°C or as high as your oven goes), a roasting tin for cooking it in and a baking stone so it fries underneath – you don't want it oily and soggy. Remember to put the salt on only just as it goes into the oven so it doesn't get the chance to dissolve and leave little scorch marks. Bake it for about 15 minutes, keeping an eye on it so it doesn't burn. With oven temperatures, whatever the dial says, gas mark or Celsius, fan-assisted or not, can throw a stick in the spokes of good baking. You can burn a loaf if you are not careful. Use temperature as a starting point and use your eyes, nose and experience for the rest. Then just serve and eat.

TECHNIQUES

If there's a breadmaking machine in the cupboard under your sink, or even on your worktop, I promise I won't hold it against you. But by and large the breadmaker is a compromise. Something that promises to mix *and* prove *and* bake might not do all of those things well. It just isn't as good as putting your own kneaded and risen dough into a really hot oven where it jumps and springs, filling your home with the aroma of fresh baking and promising good eating to come. However, a mixer with a dough hook is a great invention and could be a very worthwhile purchase.

MIXING AND KNEADING

Getting all the ingredients to come together to look like dough is one thing, but that's when you really need to knead to get it stretchy. If you are doing this by hand, then once the ingredients have come together in the bowl, scrape it out on to the worktop and start kneading. Kneading is all about getting energy into dough to enhance its elasticity. It doesn't matter that much how you do it. I use the palm of my hand and a good work surface, and I just lean into it, pushing the dough away, then roll it back on itself and lean into it again. A bit of turning now and then, but mostly leaning into it and pulling it back. You can't really overknead by hand, but you can underknead. You mustn't wuss out at this stage, because then the dough won't develop its potential. With an underdeveloped dough, the carbon dioxide given off by the yeast will simply escape, as though from a sponge, and then you end up with a brick-like loaf. If you develop the gluten, the dough becomes elastic. It will hold on to the air, and rise better, and keep its shape. Most doughs need a good 15 minutes of kneading by hand, but this depends on your strength and the amount of energy you can put into your dough.

If you are using a mixer with a dough hook, all this will be achieved in about 10 minutes and you won't even get your hands sticky. I really appreciate these, especially after having recently kneaded 15 stone of dough by hand. It took two hours and was back-breaking. A mixer at home is a great thing. At home, I weigh dough into the mixing bowl, mix it all in one, then stop the machine a couple of minutes early to finish the kneading off by hand, because I do love the feel of dough, and I get to tell whether it's a bit tight or a bit wet. Then again, if you want to take some time out from your working week to knead dough for 15 minutes, then great. It's a brilliant stress-buster.

RISING AND PROVING

Rising and proving are when the yeast gets to do its work. If you've kneaded your bread well, it will rise. As it does so, the dough will gain in strength and flavour. (To extend that process, you can make the overnight dough, where over 8 to 12 hours, depending on the time of year and the warmth of the air, the bread develops really great flavour.) The first rise in this book is done in the bowl in which you made the dough – to cut down on washing-up – which you then need to cover. The second rise is when you've shaped the loaf into whatever form you want, whether in a tin or a basket. 'Knocking back' is nothing more than what happens naturally when you scrape a dough out of a bowl on to the work surface and form it into a loaf. You lose some of the air from the first rise and you get the dough ready for the second rise. After the second rise, it's ready for the oven. Knowing when the dough is ready is one of the challenges of baking.

There's a curve with underproved at one end and overproved at the other, with an area in the centre that's fine, and a sweet spot in the very middle that's just right. Much as I'd love to come round to everyone's house and show them what it is, you have to suss this out for yourself. This is how. The first few times you make a tin loaf, weigh the dough piece. If you are using a small loaf tin (a 1-pound tin), you'll need about 450g. For a large loaf tin (a 2-pound tin), you'll need about 900g. The important thing is to use the same tin and the same weight of dough each time. You'll almost certainly have to cut off a piece of dough to get the right weight, but that's fine because you can use that piece for something else, say a little roll. So let's say you rise it until the crest of the loaf just reaches the top of the tin, and then you bake it, but you find that doesn't work out quite right. The loaf was pinched and tight, or it burst out of shape in the oven. Then you know it was underproved. The second time you leave it longer and let it rise high above the top of the tin, into a muffin top, which then collapses in the oven. This time you know it was overproved. The third time you let the dough rise to a level between the previous two, and it's perfect. Three goes and you've nailed it. Not bad for a beginner.

In short: for the first rise, you mix the dough, knead it, put it back in the bowl, cover it; the dough relaxes, you relax, it develops flavour and gets stronger. Then you take it out, it gets knocked back, and you shape it into the loaf you want, and then it has its second rise (many bakers call the second rise the 'proof'). Temperature is key to how long your dough will take to rise and, as a rule, warm is good. I always put the dough on top of the oven for the second rise. The oven is warming up; it's a good place for the dough to be.

COVERING

If you leave dough exposed, it develops a thick skin, which will give it a dull finish. To prevent that happening, cover the dough when you've finished kneading it. It also helps to work somewhere warm and draught-free. My favourite dough cover is a shower cap, the disposable sort you get free in hotels. It's elasticated so it goes easily over a bowl, you can reuse it, and it's got space for the dough to rise into. The next best thing is cling film, but when you stretch film over the bowl there's less room for expansion, and the dough might rise and stick to it. A damp tea towel is the traditional method but when the dough touches the fabric it sticks and it's difficult to get off.

SHAPING

Weigh your dough piece first. Then hold the lump of stretchy dough between your hands and bounce and flex it into a long piece the length of your forearm and hand. Put it down in front of you and fold it in thirds, from the outside in, until you have a neat, three-layer stack. Without moving it, knuckle the dough down on the edge nearest to you to seal the three layers. Then, working from the far side and using both hands, gently roll the layered dough towards you with your fingers while pushing back on the inside with your thumbs, until you've got a neat shape on top. The dough needs to be tight, but not so tight that it tears. At this point the dough will have a very fine, flexible skin around it. We've prevented this skin from getting thick by keeping it covered as much as possible. Now we fold over and tuck in the ends of the dough, gently stretching its fine skin – think of the skin of a balloon – so the dough holds itself well. A tightly moulded loaf will rise more evenly and better.

Have your tin or proving basket in front of you; you are aiming to have a moulded piece of dough of about the same length. You don't want to have to bunch it up or stretch it to fit. Put it seam-side down in a tin, but seam-side up in a proving basket because you'll invert it on to the baking tray when it's ready for the oven.

SCORING

Your signature, and your flair. You don't *have* to do it. But a well-cut loaf will have a beautiful shape and a lot of baking is about making something look attractive. If you're not sure, don't do it. And don't overdo it either. Anything too intricate won't work. You need to use a really sharp knife and to give the dough a purposeful slash (or three) without the risen loaf collapsing.

HEAT

If you put a loaf on a hot baking stone on a hot rack in an oven as hot as it will go, the loaf will react violently to the temperature: it jumps and springs, especially when it's in a tin, and it develops a beautiful shape with a perfect crust. This is called 'oven spring' and it's a good thing. So bake bread as hot as possible. The exceptions are sweet loaves, in which the sugar could burn. An oven temperature of 230/240°C (Gas 9) is appropriate for most breads; 210°C (Gas 6½) is for breads containing sugar. Baking on a falling heat is the general rule. So, put the dough in hot to get spring and crust, then check mid-bake, or after 10 minutes, and nudge the temperature down to ensure the heat gets right into the loaf (especially useful in a big loaf). All ovens vary in their highest temperature and the accuracy of their gauges. You need to know your oven.

STEAMING

Steaming creates an intensity of heat, a bit like when you pour water over the coals in a sauna, and this can help to get better oven spring and a better crust to your loaf. It's a small difference, but all these things – hot oven, baking stone, steam – add up. There are a few ways of getting steam into the oven. In an Aga, just chuck in a mugful of water in the bottom, with the dough sitting on a stone on a rack halfway up. Close the door and the whole thing whistles and steams like billy-o. In other ovens, put a dish of water into the bottom while the oven is heating up so that it creates steam. Or spritz a loaf with water just before it goes in. After 10 minutes or so, open the door to let the steam out. If you keep baking in a steamy environment the result is a chewy loaf, which is fine for some breads, like pumpernickel or bagels, but not the ones in this book.

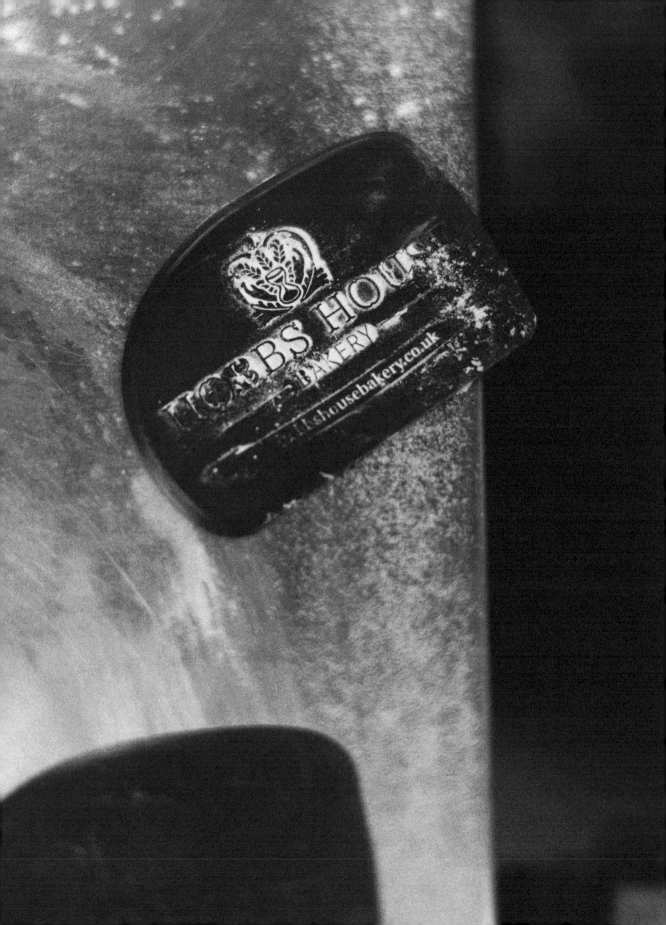

KIT

Until we've all evolved into having dough-scraper hands, I strongly recommend you get one. We do a very nice scraper with our crest on at Hobbs House!

DOUGH SCRAPER

Never bake without this indispensable bit of kit, without doubt the next best thing to the oven. A good scraper fits neatly in the hand. Its curved edge is shaped to get dough out of mixing bowls, and its sharp edge is for dividing dough and scraping a floury table. Also useful to clear an icy windscreen.

BENCH OR WORK SURFACE

This should be solid, easy to clean, and at a comfortable height. My preference is for wood. Beech is good because it has a very close grain; it's easy to maintain and great to work on.

APRON

If you're working with flour and passion, you're going to end up wearing some ingredients. It makes sense to dress for the occasion and put an apron on. They also double up as a useful thing to carry hot baked goods in.

DIGITAL SCALES

Water doesn't have to be measured by volume, it can be weighed instead. This is where digital scales come in useful. I put the mixing bowl on the digital scales, set to zero, weigh in the dry ingredients, set to zero again, then weigh the water in (1 millilitre is 1 gram, 1 litre is 1 kilogram). The same goes for milk, etc. Then, with all the ingredients accurately weighed in, bosh, off you go!

PROVING BASKET

Useful and beautiful, a proving basket will provide a soft dough with support while it rises; do use it for serving your bread in, too. Should the recipe call for a proving basket and you don't have one, just bake the dough in a tin, seam-side down. At Hobbs House we use hand-made birchwood baskets. Birchwood is not just beautiful, it allows the dough to breathe. To prevent dough sticking to the basket, dust it generously with a handful of flour before putting in your loaf. Never wash a proving basket.

TINS

Loaf tins are typically based around old sizes of 1-pound (450g) and 2-pound (900g) loaves, though you will find many varieties of size and shape. The best thing is to get a good quality, heavy one, and to stay with it and learn how to use it. Non-stick can be good, but then you don't get nice corners and sharp edges, like you do with a seamed tin that needs seasoning. To season a tin, brush it with vegetable oil, inside and out, then bake it in a hot oven on its own. Do that a couple of times when it's new, and then every now and again during the first few months of its life, if it needs it. Be warned that seasoning creates a lot of smoke and is sure to set your detector off. If you can, do it outside on a campfire or barbecue. With continued use, over time the tin goes black. In this state, it absorbs heat much quicker, and doesn't stick so much. Having a tin like this is the sign of a committed home baker.

A high-sided roasting tin (a good 5cm deep) is very useful for focaccia and rolls. Its high sides mean you can cover it in cling film and whatever is inside can rise without coming into contact with – and sticking to – the film.

BAKING STONE

A baking stone is a very worthwhile investment. It traps heat in the oven and gives loaves a spring and lift during baking as well as properly done bottoms and perfect crusts. A baking stone should live in the oven and will stain and darken to black in time, making it even better. Scrub in warm soapy water to remove burnt-on detritus. If you don't have a baking stone, use a heavy metal tray; cover it with baking paper and bake directly onto it.

DOUGH KNIFE

A short, razor-sharp serrated knife with a good grip enables you to give your loaves clean, snagless signature cuts.

OVEN GLOVES

You need good oven gloves. We have tried every glove going, time and time again, until we settled on the hessian glove. Hessian is naturally good for heat protection, and has flexibility and grip.

ALL READY TO GO?

1 Find yourself some time, clear yourself a space, gather all the ingredients and kit, then commence.

2 Wake the dried yeast in a little of the tepid water you are going to use. Whisk with a fork into the bottom of the jug until the lumps have gone. Weigh salt and flour directly into the bowl on the scales, then offer the yeast into the mix. If you have fresh yeast, weigh in double the amount. Weigh in the rest of the tepid water.

3 Right, get mixing. If you have a mixer, blend the ingredients on slowest speed for 2 minutes to save your kitchen from a flour storm, then crank her up to halfway and knead the heck out of the dough for 8–10 minutes. If you're doing this by hand, mix the ingredients together in the large mixing bowl with one hand. Save the other hand for later; it can hold the bowl for now. Once the ingredients have come together, use the scraper to tease it out of the bowl on to the worktop and knead it like a baker for 15 minutes.

4 Put the dough into the bowl, cover it and leave to double in size, or for an hour, whichever comes first.

5 On the worktop, gently hand mould the dough. Cover again and goad the loaf to rise a final time in a warm place. On top of the oven while it's cranking up is good. If you have a baking stone make sure it's in there. When the crest of the loaf makes an appearance above the tin or basket, it's time to get the oven dish with water into the oven to make some steam.

6 Steaming? Then GO! Get the dough in and DO NOT DISTURB for 10 minutes. Now take the bowl of steam carefully out and get a sniff of that bread, see how it's sprung. Ace. Nudge the heat down a bit.

7 Check the loaf after it's had half an hour; if the bottom is golden and sounds hollow when tapped, you're done. (Tip the loaf out of its tin to check its bottom – use hessian gloves.) Cool out of the tin.

WHITE
AND
WHOLEMEAL

AIN'T NOTHING FINER THAN SHARING A FRESHLY BAKED, HAND-MADE LOAF

We all love to share a meal with people we like. The root of the word 'companion' means 'with bread'. Eating good food, something with a story, with a nice bit of cheese perhaps, or some home-grown salad, a neighbour's eggs, a bottle or two of real ale, the pop and first sip of a great glass of wine, clinked together with a 'cheers', is a daily celebration of life itself. Real bread, made with good flour, not over-pumped with water, but given time to rise and develop a good flavour and made with care, can be the heart of an occasion. From the first crunch of a fine crust to the fingertip retrieval of the final crumb, any time spent with friends and food is encouraged along when real bread is shared. We're learning that the best thing since sliced bread is real bread, and the ultimate expression of this is in baking your own. It's a hugely rewarding habit, affording us the opportunity to connect with an ancient process that requires very little investment of time or equipment. White and wholemeal bread are the keystones. There's very little to go wrong and they are relatively easy to handle. Once you've mastered these, the whole world of baking is open to you. This is the place to start.

WHITE DOUGH: TIN LOAF

• MAKES 1 LARGE LOAF •

The foundation stone for great home-baking. This recipe for one large loaf is basic, simple, reliable, forgiving and extraordinarily versatile. To get the best out of your loaf, keep it in a linen or paper bag in a bread bin. Or, once cooled, slice and freeze it in a freezer bag. Enjoy your tin loaf as toast, sandwiches or soldiers, or in any of the tasty recipes in this chapter.

INGREDIENTS	KIT	Large loaf tin (900g)
560g strong white flour	Set of scales, preferably digital	Fork
10g sea salt	Measuring jug	Oven: 230/240°C at baking time
300ml tepid water	Large mixing bowl or mixer with dough hook	Baking stone* and plastic scraper
20ml rapeseed oil		Oven dish for steam*
5g dried yeast (or 10g fresh yeast if you can get it)	Cling film or a disposable shower cap	*optional

1 Weigh the flour and salt into a big bowl. Measure the water and oil into a jug. With a fork, stir the yeast into the water and empty the jug into the bowl. Alternatively, weigh the water (300g), oil (20g) and yeast directly into the bowl. Mix the ingredients to bring them all together, then turn out the dough on to the work surface and knead by hand for 15 minutes. If you are using a mixer with a dough hook, let it bring all the ingredients together and do the kneading for you: this takes about 10 minutes all together. Once you have a smooth and elastic dough, nestle it back into the bowl and cover it with cling film or a shower cap. Leave it in a warm place to grow to twice its size or for 1 hour (whichever is first).

2 Then, by hand, shape the dough so it fits evenly into a well-oiled large loaf tin.

3 Dust the top of the loaf with a bit of flour, cover the tin, and leave in a warm place to double in size or for 1 hour (whichever is first). Meanwhile, crank up the oven as high as she goes (max 240°C). Slash the top of the loaf and offer it into the HOT oven. Check it after 10 minutes and turn the oven down a notch (210°C). Take it out when it's baked and beautifully golden all over (about 30 minutes). Let the smell of freshly baked bread fill your home and share the joy of a real loaf.

Find a mill where you can collect a large sack of locally grown and stoneground flour.

Don't skimp at the kneading stage or be tempted to add more flour.

TOM'S TIPS

WHOLEMEAL DOUGH: TIN LOAF

MAKES 1 LARGE LOAF

To bake a delicious wholemeal loaf, follow the recipe on page 50, replacing the white flour with wholemeal. Wholemeal flour is more hygroscopic (thirsty) than white flour; the very dry bran in wholemeal flour has a way of continuing to absorb water long after you've finished mixing and kneading it. So, to make a moist wholemeal loaf, be prepared to weigh more water into the dough. Ten per cent extra is a good place to start, and, as flours differ one from another, you'll need to use your judgement to get a feel for the ideal dough consistency. With experience this will fast become easy.

The dough will feel more manageable after the first rise. To develop the full gluten potential in wholemeal flour you'll need to knead it for a couple of minutes longer than white. Bran tastes great in a loaf, and is probably very good for you too, but it contributes nothing to the rising of your loaf because it doesn't contain the same gluten-forming potential, so do expect less volume and rise from your wholemeal loaf than from its high-rise white brother. With the addition of enough water, however, you shouldn't expect it to be dry, heavy and brick-like. On the contrary, it should be soft, delicious and, when buttered hot from the oven, fabulous enough to win over kids and any wholemeal haters.

'Dock' the top (pierce here and there with a fork) when you put the dough in the tin to keep the crust intact when it bakes. Also, it looks pretty.

TOM'S TIPS

ESTD 1920

OVERNIGHT DOUGH: THE SHERSTON LOAF

• MAKES 1 LARGE LOAF •

This is a loaf to make the BEST TOAST IN THE WORLD! It has a lush flavour, which comes from the long, slow, overnight fermentation. Thomas Herbert, our great-grandfather, was baking at a time when yeast was expensive, so he made dough with about a tenth of the quantity used in modern, mass-produced 'bread', and left it overnight to rise. Although overnight dough bread was born out of economic necessity, it has stood the test of time. In no small part this is because it tastes so wonderful, it's a great all-rounder with a soft close texture that makes it perfect for sandwiches, and toasted it's brilliant. The tiny amount of yeast, which ensures a long slow rise, also makes this bread easier to digest for a lot of people, and it keeps fresh for longer than most other loaves.

560g strong white flour	2g dried yeast or 4g fresh	100ml milk (full-fat is best)
10g sea salt	20g fat (butter/lard/white shortening or a combination)	200ml cool water
10g sugar		

1 Mix all the ingredients together for 10 minutes in a mixer or 15 minutes by hand until you have a smooth stiff dough. Cover and leave in a cool place to rest for 2 hours. Mould to fit a large tin and then, having placed it in the tin, cover and leave overnight to rise in the fridge. In the morning (or after about 8 hours), the loaf will have risen slightly. Take it out of the fridge and put it somewhere warm to carry on rising: it could take from 1 to 3 hours. Heat the oven up to 240°C (if it doesn't go that high, then as hot as it'll go). Lightly dust the risen dough with flour and give it five slashes with a sharp knife. Steam the oven (see page 40) and bake the loaf in the tin directly on the baking stone. Remember to turn down the temperature after 10 minutes.

2 Once the loaf is baked a beautiful golden colour and rings hollow when tapped on the bottom (about 35 minutes), then take it out of the oven and cool on a wire rack.

TOM'S TIPS

A strong flour will give you the best results; a flour made with British wheat will typically give you a better flavour. The dough for this loaf is really quite firm and tight, which can make mixing and kneading hard work, but after its first rest it becomes much softer and easier to handle.

BREAD STICKS

MAKES ABOUT 2 DOZEN

Not bad for something to nibble on, and impressive in a jug, like a butt of gnarly old walking sticks, I reckon once you've mastered the white dough you should have a go at these. It's a decent bread card to have up your culinary sleeve, and an opportune prop with which to poke someone in real life you'd normally only poke on Facebook.

1 Find the largest baking tray that will fit in the oven and cover it with a sheet of baking paper. After your white dough has had its first rise (see page 50), take a piece about 500g in weight and roll it out on a floured work surface until the dough is just under a centimetre thick, spray or brush the top with water and season with seeds, za'atar or whatever you fancy (the water will help the topping to stick).

2 With a sharp knife, cut the rolled-out dough into strips and place them on the tray, stretching each one to fit. If you're feeling crazy, cut loose and pop a couple of twists into the stick. Once the tray is full, put it on the hot baking stone (230°C) and spank it in the oven for 8 minutes, or until they start to golden up. Once they are baked, let them cool properly before presenting them upright.

TOM'S TIPS

Leave a little space between each one so they can jump in size in the oven without conjoining. Out of the oven, let them cool before you stand them on end, or they'll droop. A bendy stick isn't so good for a dip. Tie a bunch together as an edible treat to take to friends instead of flowers.

SIX-SEED MALTED WHEAT

· MAKES 1 LARGE LOAF ·

This recipe is based on a new and very popular Hobbs House loaf. Generally, shoppers are either looking for a white or a brown: this is the go-to brown loaf. It's light, soft, beautiful and full of crunch, with a beguiling chewiness from the softened wheat flakes, delicious nutty seeds that make toasting it a dream, and a crust to get your teeth into. A loaf like this is a simple and wholesome everyday bread, excellent made into sandwiches, or with pâté, cheese or soup.

560g malted wheat flour	10g sea salt	385g tepid water
85g mixed seeds: I use pumpkin, millet, golden linseed, sunflower, poppy, sesame	5g dried yeast (or 10g fresh yeast if you can get it)	
	20g rapeseed or olive oil	

1 Weigh all the ingredients into a mixing bowl. Mix them all together, then turn the dough out on to the work surface and knead by hand for 15 minutes. If using a mixer with a dough hook, let it do the mixing and kneading for you: takes about 10 minutes. Once you have a smooth and elastic dough, nestle it back into the bowl and cover it with cling film or a shower cap. Leave it in a warm place to grow to twice its size or for 1 hour (whichever is first).

2 Then, by hand, shape the dough so it fits evenly into a well-floured proving basket, with the seam uppermost. Cover and leave in a warm place to double in size or for 1 hour (whichever is first).

3 Heat the oven as high as she goes (max 240°C). Turn the dough out on to a well-floured baking tray, slash the top of the loaf and offer it into the HOT oven. Check it after 10 minutes and turn the oven down a little (210°C). Take it out when it's baked and beautifully golden all over (about 30 minutes in total).

WHITE AND WHOLEMEAL

COMBINE HARVESTER

MAKES 1 LARGE LOAF

A wonderfully tasty, seedy, oaty spelt loaf. In a little under three hours, from an itching-to-bake beginning, you'll be biting into the first hot, butter-slathered, nutty, seedy, blissful slice. So clear a space and get started.

465g wholemeal spelt flour	10g sea salt	300g tepid water
50g sunflower seeds	5g dried yeast (or 10g fresh yeast if you can get it)	50g rapeseed oil
50g linseeds		50g jumbo oats

1 Weigh all the ingredients except the oats into a mixing bowl. Mix them all together, then turn the dough out on to the work surface and knead by hand for 15 minutes. If using a mixer with a dough hook, let it do the mixing and kneading for you: takes about 10 minutes. Once you have a smooth and elastic dough, quickly work the oats through. Adding the oats at the end means they don't break up and therefore give your loaf more interest and bite. Nestle the dough back into the bowl and cover it with cling film or a shower cap. Leave it in a warm place to grow to twice its size or for 1 hour (whichever is first).

2 Shape the dough to fit a tin or proving basket, as desired. Cover and leave in a warm place to double in size or for 1 hour (whichever is first).

3 Heat the oven as high as she goes (max 240°C). Turn the dough out of its proving basket on to a baking tray (or keep it in its tin) and bake in the HOT oven, checking it after 10 minutes and turning the oven down a little (210°C). Take it out when it's baked and beautifully golden all over (about 30 minutes in total).

SMOKING SQUIRREL COB

• MAKES 1 LARGE LOAF •

This is just a wee bit bonkers, but it goes to show that once you've got the basics, you can go far. This is a smoky cob loaf, squirrelling away cobnuts and elderberries, perfect for mopping up gamey juices and lush with strong cheese. The combination of oak-smoked flour and smoked sea salt gives the hint of a great autumnal bonfire to the loaf, and a whiff of it baking is as lovely as sniffing a woolly jumper after a good campfire. The cobnuts are totally worth the effort and will reward your teeth with a super beautiful crunch that certainly brings out my inner squirrel. The elderberries will aid fermentation and bleed into the dough, staining it and studding it like a fruitful hedgerow. The elderberries are also tasty sweet and nutritious. Good malted wheat flour, regular sea salt and hazelnuts can be used if you don't have the ingredients above. Bright eyes and bushy tails!

400g oak-smoked stoneground strong malted blend flour (Bacheldre water mill)	pinch of Halen Môn smoked sea salt	200ml warm water
	10g fresh yeast or 5g dried	100g elderberries
	20ml walnut oil	100g cobnuts, shelled

1 Weigh and mix the ingredients, keeping back the cobnuts, elderberries, and some of the flour. Knead the dough for 10 minutes, then taste for seasoning. Add the cobnuts and elderberries, working them into the dough, and gently knead for 5 minutes, adding the rest of the flour as needed. Cover the dough and give it its first rise back in the mixing bowl, as usual.

2 Once it has doubled in size (1 hour in a warm place), turn it out and mould it into a round cob shape. Place on a baking tray to prove and cover with the upturned mixing bowl. Allow to rise a second time in a warm place (1 hour, or to double size).

3 Heat the oven to 230°C. Bake for 30 minutes, or until the crust is golden and the bottom sounds hollow when tapped underneath.

TOM'S TIPS

While the loaf is still warm, brush the crust a couple of times with walnut oil for a lustrous finish, like a winning polished conker.

Try smoking your own flour and salt using the smoker on page 185: hang them from the dowel in tight-mesh muslin bags and smoke them gently for a few hours.

SANDWICHES USING WHITE TIN LOAF

BLT

FEEDS 4

This is my fall-back sandwich, one that everyone turns to when given too much choice. But it's so often done badly and ends up disappointing. Done right, however, it is a thing to behold and devour.

8 slices freshly baked white bread, still just warm	2 vine tomatoes at room temperature	pepper
	1 baby gem lettuce	
8 slices dry-cure back bacon, rindless	50g mayonnaise (for home-made, see page 90)	

1 Heat a frying pan and fry off the bacon. I like my bacon to be crispy but with a little squish in the middle: about 3 minutes on each side. Remove and drain on some kitchen paper towel.

2 Slice the tomatoes quite thinly and use the ends for something else. Cut the leaves off the baby gem, and wash and dry it.

3 Now assemble the sandwich. Spread some mayo on the bottom layer of bread. Next add the bacon followed by the tomatoes. A pinch of pepper on the tomato does wonders. Finish with the baby gem and the top slice of bread. Give it a firm squash down and eat before the bread and bacon go soggy.

HENRY'S TIPS

Tomatoes will make a sandwich go soggy, so use the lettuce as a barrier.

You get more bacon for your money with dry-cure; it doesn't leak water when fried.

A spoonful of mustard mixed into the mayo adds a little kick.

CHIP BUTTIES WITH ONCE-BOILED TWICE-FRIED CHIPS

FEEDS 4

Chip butties are beige food at its greatest, and the ultimate hunger-slayer. Good soft white bread, smothered in salty butter, with crispy and fluffy deep-fried chips. It is one of the best sandwiches to eat after a long day; double carbs is doubly good in my view. A soft white tin loaf, freshly baked, is best, and you can't beat home-made once-boiled, twice-fried chips. They require a bit of preparation but are so worth it: soft and fluffy in the centre with a glass-like crispiness on the outside.

FOR THE CHIPS
2kg Maris Piper potatoes
2 litres of veg oil

FOR THE BUTTIES
8 slices freshly baked white bread
best salted butter you can find

1 Peel and wash the spuds, then chip them. I generally like my chips quite chunky, but for a chip butty you want something just larger than a French fry. So cut the potatoes lengthways into 1cm slices. Cut them across the middle if they are long. Pile up a few slices then slice them into 1cm chips. Go for the rustic look, keeping the edges rough.

2 Place in a pan of cold water and bring to the boil. Allow to simmer for a few minutes, but keep a close eye. We want the chip to start to cook on the outside, but not completely cook through and turn to mash. It is a fine line. Using a slotted spoon, carefully lift the chips out and into a colander, shake them up to rough the edges while still hot. Pour onto a tray and leave to cool completely.

3 Heat a fat-fryer to 130°C, or warm up the vegetable oil in a pan using a probe to gauge the temperature accurately. Fry the chips in small batches for 5 minutes, or until they are cooked through and the edges have sealed up but not gone too crispy or gained any colour. Place on a tray and cool completely once again.

4 When ready for butties, heat a fat-fryer to 190°C. You might not need all the chips at once, so fry as many as you'd like, giving them just 2 minutes until they are golden in colour and crispy as anything. Remove from the oil and drain on some paper. Slather the bread with butter and assemble your butties. Squash the bread down into the chips, share out and devour.

FISH FINGER SARNIES WITH TARTARE SAUCE

── FEEDS 4 ──

If chip butties are the king of beige, fish finger sarnies are the queen. Home-made fish fingers are super-easy to make and freeze well, so make a large batch and keep them for a rainy day. Push the boat out and make your own mayonnaise as well.

8 slices of white bread or 4 white baps (such as our Ultimate Burger Baps, on page 182)	50g milk	1 tbsp finely chopped capers
	30g flour	8 cocktail gherkins (cornichons), finely chopped
	100g breadcrumbs	
200g fillet of white fish, such as cod, pollock or whiting, skinned	1 baby gem lettuce	1 small shallot, finely diced
	FOR THE TARTARE SAUCE:	50g mayonnaise (for home-made, see page 90)
salt and pepper	1 tsp finely chopped parsley	
2 eggs	1 tsp finely chopped tarragon	salt and pepper

1 Slice the fish into thin strips, about 1cm wide. Season with salt and pepper.

2 Whisk the eggs and milk together. Dust the fish in the flour and shake the excess off. Dip in the egg and milk, then roll in the breadcrumbs. Dip back into the egg and again through the breadcrumbs. Place in the fridge to firm up.

3 To make the tartare sauce, stir all the chopped ingredients into the mayonnaise. Season to taste. It should be quite coarse, thick and pungent.

4 Heat a fat-fryer to 170°C (or warm the vegetable oil in a pan using a probe to gauge the temperature accurately) and cook the fish fingers for 5 minutes, until brown and crispy. The fish will cook quite quickly, and it's better to be just done than dry

and mushy. Remove and season. Spread the bread liberally with tartare sauce. Add a layer of fish fingers and a few leaves of baby gem. Give the whole thing a quick squash and eat whilst looking at a rainy window and thinking the world isn't so bad when you've got a fish finger sarnie.

Tail ends of fish are cheaper and work perfectly for these.

A few leaves of baby gem lettuce add a bit of health and crunch to the finished sarnie.

HENRY'S TIPS

WHITE AND WHOLEMEAL

70

WHITE BREAD TOASTIES

There is something very nostalgic about a Breville toastie machine, producing a crispy triangle of squashed bread with a molten centre of oozing goodness. As a child I used to make dangerously hot cheese and chutney toasties at my granny's house. On reflection, hot chutney doesn't sound quite so appealing, but there was definitely something special about those golden beauties. Here are some fun ideas that take the humble toastie to new heights. You can make these even if you don't have an old Breville to dust down. Just fry the toasties on both sides in butter, flattening with a spatula as you go.

FOIE GRAS AND GUINEA FOWL

MAKES 2 TOASTIES

Unctuous duck livers paired with gamey guinea fowl spiked with a pinch of tarragon – a taste of luxury. This hot beauty first came about using the leftovers of a Sunday lunch my friend Rhys Bennett cooked for me.

4 slices of white tin loaf, crusts removed	1 tbsp butter, preferably smoked	1 egg yolk
	100g foie gras	1 tsp chopped tarragon
1 garlic clove, finely diced	100g cooked guinea fowl, roughly chopped	salt and pepper
1 shallot, finely diced		15g melted butter

1 Heat a small pan and gently sweat the garlic and shallot in the butter. When soft, set aside to cool.

2 Place the foie gras, guinea fowl, egg yolk, tarragon and shallot and garlic mixture in a Kitchen Aid or other such mixer and gently beat to form a stiff paste. Season.

3 Scoop a ball and place in the middle of each bottom layer of bread, add a lid and squeeze the edges down. Brush with melted butter, place in the hot Breville and cook for 5 minutes or until crispy.

HENRY'S TIPS

Smoke the butter in your smoker (see page 185). Wrap it in muslin, hang from the pole and smoke really gently for 1–2 hours. It will taste better the next day as the flavour mellows. If you can't get fresh foie gras, foie gras pâté is fine. Duck liver parfait also works (see page 179).

BEAUFORT CHEESE AND SMOKED HAM (THE 'CHAP')

MAKES 2 TOASTIES

A classic: the rich caramel-salty cheese of the Savoie region with smoky ham hot and smeared in Dijon mustard is up there with the best. Not so much a recipe as a rite of passage for any young squirt on the quest for culinary adventure beyond beans on toast.

4 slices of white tin loaf, crusts removed	4 slices of Beaufort or other Gruyère-style cheese	2 slices of smoked ham
		15g melted butter

1 This hardly feels like it needs instructions, but for those in the dark: place a piece of Beaufort on each bread base followed by the ham, slap on another slice of cheese followed by the top layer of bread. Squish the edges of the toastie together, brush with melted butter for shine and crunch, and place in the grooves of a hot Breville. Cook for 5 minutes or until crispy and molten hot. Eat straight away or once you can handle the hot cheese. I like mine slathered in Dijon mustard.

HENRY'S TIPS

To take this to new heights, make a thick béchamel sauce and grate in the cheese. This makes the toastie even more gooey and rich. Or top with a fried egg, and voilà – croque madame.

WHITE AND WHOLEMEAL

WILD MUSHROOM AND BUFFALO MOZZARELLA

MAKES 2 TOASTIES

Earthy, savoury wild mushrooms with mild, creamy, stringy mozzarella: what a great match. Sometimes I like to be a little naughty and put a few drips of truffle oil in, just to give it that nasal hit. Adding bits of crispy bacon is not a bad idea either, but for now I'm keeping this strictly veggie.

4 slices of white tin loaf, crusts removed

200g wild mushrooms – I like trompettes de la morte ('trumpets of death')

1 tbsp olive oil

salt and pepper

1 tsp chopped flat-leaf parsley

½ tsp truffle oil (optional)

1 ball of buffalo mozzarella

15g melted butter

1 Wash and pick through the mushrooms, removing all dirt, leaves and moss. Dry thoroughly and set aside.

2 Heat a frying pan and fry the mushrooms in the oil; when they start to give off moisture, add salt and pepper. After 2–3 minutes, remove from the heat and stir through the chopped parsley and truffle oil, if using. Drain the mozzarella from its water cocoon and tear into small pieces.

3 Spoon a little wild mushroom into the middle of each bottom layer of bread. Add some mozzarella and sprinkle with a little salt and pepper as the cheese is quite mild. Squish the top layer of bread on and crimp the edges. Brush with melted butter, place in a hot Breville and cook till golden: around 5 minutes.

Portobello or chestnut mushrooms are just as good if you can't source wild ones: fry well to intensify the flavours. If you have picked your own mushrooms, make sure you know what you are eating. Some of them are killers!

HENRY'S TIPS

PEANUT BUTTER, BANANA AND CHOCOLATE FLAKE

MAKES 2 TOASTIES

When I was a wee slip of a lad, I used to bake a sliced banana in the skin with chocolate in between the slices. I ate this if ever I was starting to feel poorly and it always made me better. Use chunky peanut butter for the extra texture. Ripe bananas are a must here.

4 slices of white tin loaf, crusts removed	1 ripe banana	15g sugar
	4 chocolate flakes	
4 tbsp chunky peanut butter	15g melted butter	

1 Spread peanut butter on 2 slices. Don't go quite to the edges. Peel and slice the banana and place on top. Top with 2 flakes on each slice. Cover with the remaining white slices, squeeze down and seal the edges.

2 Brush with the melted butter and sprinkle with the sugar. Put in a hot Breville and cook for 5 minutes till golden and molten.

WHITE AND WHOLEMEAL

WORLD OF BREADCRUMBS

Bread a few days old is best for breadcrumbs. Cut the crust off, slice
the bread, leave to dry, then either process, or crumb by hand for as
long as you have the patience. Most of the fried-breadcrumb recipes
are better with hard crumbs, while the Queen of Puddings is
better with soft (so use fresher bread).

WIENER SCHNITZEL

• FEEDS 2 •

This dish takes me straight back to college, though I believe we made them with turkey, which is just wrong. Try to use rose veal from a local supplier rather than Dutch veal. We stock rose veal regularly. I like my schnitzel either with a potato salad or in a sandwich.

2 veal escalopes	2 eggs	oil and butter
salt and pepper	50ml milk	1 lemon
30g flour	100g breadcrumbs	

1 Place the veal escalopes on a flat surface and bash thin with a rolling pin. Season with a little salt and pepper.

2 Dust the escalopes in the flour and shake the excess off. Whisk the eggs and milk together and dip the veal in. Then pat with breadcrumbs. Dip again into the egg and back into the crumbs. Place in the fridge to firm up.

3 Heat a large pan and add a splash of oil and a knob of butter. Gently fry the wiener schnitzel for 3 minutes on each side till brown and crisp. Remove and serve with a lemon wedge.

HENRY'S TIPS

If you can't get hold of veal, or have an issue with it, pork or chicken is fine. For a potato salad, boil some new potatoes (I like Jersey royals or pink fir apple potatoes), then mix with a dollop of crème fraîche, some seasoning, chopped chives and a slug of olive oil. Eat while still warm.

CHICKEN KIEV

⸺ FEEDS 2 ⸺

These have been a massive hit at my butchery. I have memories of getting them from a fancy supermarket on a Friday night once in a blue moon. The way the garlic butter would ooze out used to fill me with delight.

2 garlic cloves	1 lemon	2 eggs
120g butter	salt and pepper	50ml milk
small bunch of parsley, coarsely chopped	2 skinless chicken breasts	100g breadcrumbs
	30g flour	

1 Crush the garlic into a food processor, add the butter and the coarsely chopped parsley. Zest the lemon in, and add a pinch of salt and pepper. Blend till you have a smooth green butter. Remove and set aside.

2 Take the chicken breast and turn it upside down. Lift up the inner fillet, then using a sharp knife make a small slit on the other side into the thick part of the fillet to make another flap. Open the two flaps to give you a butterflied chicken breast. Season with a little salt and pepper. Spoon a generous amount of the green butter in, and close the flaps to seal. Place in the fridge for 1 hour to firm up.

3 Now to 'pane', or breadcrumb: dust the breast in the flour and shake off any excess. Whisk the milk and eggs together and season with a pinch of salt. Dip the Kiev into the egg and then into the crumbs, and then repeat the egg and crumb dipping once more. Place back into the fridge to firm up again.

4 Heat the oven to 180°C. Heat a large frying pan and add a splash of oil and a knob of butter. Place the Kievs in and brown carefully on each side. When golden, place into an oven dish inside a piece of foil. Pour any pan butter over the top and bake for 20 minutes or until done. Slice in half and serve, pouring any escaped butter back on the top.

HENRY'S TIPS

Try changing the butter. Tarragon, anchovy, truffle oil or spices all add interest to the dish. Chips or mash is a good pairing. Use free-range chicken breasts: they are firmer and better.

WHITE AND WHOLEMEAL

SCOTCH EGGS

━━━━ • MAKES 6 • ━━━━

These little rascals have been following me around for the last few years.
I've gained something of a reputation for them, and people apparently still
ask for them in the Coach and Horses, the London pub where I used to be chef.
Their recent renaissance must be because mass-produced ones are so bad that
anything home-made is a million times improved. Here is my classic recipe.
Serve warm with a lick of English mustard. A hard-to-beat portable snack.

6 free-range eggs	¼ tsp mace	**FOR THE COATING:**
knob of butter	pinch of cayenne	2 eggs
50g shallot, finely chopped	1 tbsp English mustard	50ml milk
150g minced pork shoulder	4 sage leaves, finely chopped	50g flour
150g minced pork belly	salt and pepper	100g breadcrumbs
1 sprig of thyme	vegetable oil for frying	

1 Bring a big pan of water to a
simmer, carefully lower in the
eggs and cook for 8 minutes. The eggs
should be slightly runny in the middle.
Run under a cold tap until they are
completely cold and carefully peel
off the shells.

2 Melt the butter in a pan and cook
the shallot until soft. Mix with
the other ingredients, seasoning well.

3 In a piece of cling film, pat out a
piece of the sausage-meat mixture
large enough to envelop an egg. Put
the egg in the middle and, using the
cling film, fold it around the egg so it
is completely covered. Remove the cling
film and mould with your hands so there
is an even thickness all the way around.
Repeat with all the other eggs and put
into the fridge to firm up.

4 For the coating, whisk the eggs
and milk with a pinch of salt. Dust
the sausage-coated eggs in the flour
and shake off the excess, then dip into
the egg mix and then through the
breadcrumbs. Dip back through the
eggs and into the crumb mix again.
Place into the fridge to firm up.

5 Heat a fat-fryer to 185°C (or warm
up vegetable oil in a pan using
a probe to gauge the temperature
accurately) and the oven to 200°C.
Brown the Scotch eggs for 2 minutes
in the fryer then place in the oven
for 10 minutes to warm through.

THE RAJ EGG

MAKES 4

This innovation came to me in a eureka moment. Smoked haddock kedgeree wrapped around a boiled egg and deep-fried – what's not to like?

4 free-range eggs	1 onion	**FOR THE COATING:**
400ml milk	30g butter	2 eggs
1 bay leaf	80g risotto rice	50ml milk
pinch each of ground coriander, cumin, turmeric and nutmeg	1 tbsp chopped parsley	1 tsp turmeric
	salt and pepper	100g breadcrumbs
150g piece of smoked haddock	vegetable oil for frying	30g flour

1 Prepare the eggs as in step 1 of Scotch Eggs on page 86.

2 Pour the first measure of milk into a pan with the bay and spices. Bring to the heat and put the smoked haddock in. Take off the heat and leave the haddock to poach. After 5 minutes, remove the haddock with a slotted spoon, flake the flesh and set aside. Keep the milk.

3 Chop the onion finely. Melt the butter in a saucepan and sweat the onion gently. After 3 minutes, add the risotto rice. Stir constantly as the rice briefly fries. Ladle the milk in one scoop at a time. Keep stirring as the milk is absorbed into the rice. The whole process will take about 15 minutes. If the milk runs out before the rice is cooked, keep going with some fresh milk. For this recipe you want to slightly overcook the rice as this makes it easier to mould later on.

4 When the rice is cooked, stir in the flakes of haddock and chopped parsley. Season to taste. It should be rich, smoky, fishy and spicy. Allow to completely cool before assembling.

5 Take a small ball of haddock rice, say 80g. Place a piece of cling film on a table and pat out an even disc of mixture about 5mm thick. Pop the egg into the middle and gently bring the cling film over, wrapping the egg in the haddock rice. Now, with quick light hands, smooth the mixture evenly around the egg. When the Raj looks all smooth and egg-like, place in the fridge to firm up.

6 For the coating, whisk the eggs with the milk. Add a pinch of salt. Mix the turmeric into the breadcrumbs for the authentic Raj look. Dust the Raj egg in the flour and shake the excess off. Dip into the egg and roll in the breadcrumbs, dip again in the egg and back through the crumbs. Place back in the fridge.

7 Heat a fat-fryer to 185°C (or warm up vegetable oil in a pan using a probe to gauge the temperature accurately) and the oven to 180°C. Brown the Raj egg in the fryer for 2 minutes till brown and crispy, then place in the oven for 10 minutes to warm through. Serve with curry sauce (see page 90).

THE CROQUE MADAME EGG

━━━━━ • MAKES 6 • ━━━━━

This oozing, exploding cheesy delight comes courtesy of my dear friend Chris Redmond. Inspired by a Croque Madame cheese toastie, these beauties have all the same ingredients, but so much more pleasure.

6 free-range eggs	50g Gruyère, grated	**FOR THE COATING:**
300ml milk	30g ham, finely chopped	2 eggs
1 bay leaf, 1 clove, ¼ onion	1 tsp Dijon mustard	50ml milk
30g butter	salt and pepper	30g flour
30g flour		100g breadcrumbs

1 Prepare the eggs as in step 1 of Scotch Eggs on page 86.

2 Pour the milk into a pan and add the bay, clove and onion; heat and infuse for 5 minutes. In a separate pan, melt the butter and stir in the flour (to make a roux). Strain the milk and slowly beat into the roux, letting the mixture gradually thicken. Keep adding the milk until the béchamel sauce is thick and glossy. Cook gently for 10 minutes.

3 Stir the Gruyère, ham and mustard into the béchamel. Season to taste.

4 Lay a piece of cling film on a tray, pour the béchamel on top and spread evenly. Lay another piece of cling film neatly on top and put the tray in the fridge for 2 hours to set.

5 The next bit is quite fiddly. Take the tray out of the fridge and remove the top layer of film. Cut a largish disc out, big enough to envelop an egg. Pop an egg in the middle and wrap the béchamel mixture carefully over the egg, using the cling film to help get it in place. When the result is smooth, put the coated egg in the fridge to firm up and carry on with the rest of the eggs.

6 Whisk the eggs for the coating with the milk and a pinch of salt. Dust the Croque eggs in the flour and shake off the excess. Dip into the egg mixture then roll in the breadcrumbs. Dip again into the egg and back through the crumbs. Firm up in the fridge.

7 Heat a fat-fryer to 185°C (or warm up vegetable oil in a pan using a probe to gauge the temperature accurately) and the oven to 180°C. Brown the eggs for 2 minutes in the fryer then place in the oven for 10 minutes. Don't eat straight away on caution of boiling cheesy sauce. Devour while still warm.

WHITE AND WHOLEMEAL

HAGGIS SCOTCH EGG

According to Fortnum and Mason, who claim to have invented the Scotch egg, the original included haggis in the sausage meat. It is surprisingly good, so give it a go.

Follow the classic Scotch egg recipe on page 86, but instead of using English mustard, sage and 150g pork belly, use 150g cooked haggis.

BLACK PUDDING SCOTCH EGG

The black pudding adds a certain chocolateyness to this tasty snack. A boudin noir-style black pudding works best because it blends better than rusk-heavy varieties.

Again, proceed as in the classic recipe on page 86, but replace 50g of the pork mince with 50g black pudding, and instead of the mustard and sage, use 1 tbsp chopped parsley. Beat until you have a uniform colour.

MAYONNAISE

Whisk 2 egg yolks with 1 teaspoon each of white wine vinegar and Dijon mustard. Use a round-bottomed bowl to get good whisking action, and have a jug containing 200ml vegetable oil to hand. Slowly trickle in the oil, whisking all the time – put the bowl on a folded-up tea towel if it helps with stability. When the mixture is really thick, whisk in a spoon of water to thin it slightly, then carry on whisking in the remaining oil. Season. Home-made mayonnaise lasts for about 5 days in the fridge. Once you've mastered making your own, it leads to countless other possibilities. Think tartare, anchovy, garlic, herb, coronation…

CURRY SAUCE

For that authentic chip-shop curry-sauce moment, make your own. Fry a little curry powder (to taste) in oil with finely chopped fresh ginger and chopped apple. Make a paste with cornflour and apple juice, and stir into the spice and apple mixture. Simmer until nicely thickened. Especially good with the Raj egg.

BREAD SAUCE WITH ROAST CHICKEN

• FEEDS 4 TO 6 •

A good bread sauce for chicken is more important than gravy to me. If you buy a decent free-range chicken and cook it with plenty of butter and lemon, it makes its own sauce in the pan. So use leftover bread to make a sauce with that nursery feel. There is just something quite comforting about the whole situation.

BREAD SAUCE FOR A LARGE CHICKEN

20g butter

1 small onion, diced

1 pint of whole (full-fat) milk

1 clove

1 sprig of thyme

1 bay leaf

300g fresh white breadcrumbs

salt and cracked black pepper

1 Melt the butter in a pan, add the onion and gently soften for about 5 minutes. Pour in the milk, clove, thyme and bay. Bring just to the boil, then remove and leave to infuse for 30 minutes to 1 hour. Carefully spoon out the herbs and clove. Add the breadcrumbs and heat again till thick and lumpy. Season with plenty of salt and cracked black pepper. If you like a smoother sauce, give it a quick pulse in a food processor. If you like it thicker or thinner, adjust the milk to your taste.

When in season, a handful of chopped wild garlic (ramsons) stirred into the bread sauce at the end is lovely.

HENRY'S TIPS

ROAST CHICKEN

1 large free-range chicken,
local if possible, about 2kg

salt and pepper

50g butter, softened

1 lemon

1 bulb of garlic

1 sprig of thyme

FOR THE SAUCE:

1 small glass of white wine (about 125ml)

1 tbsp flour

a little vegetable water or stock

pinch of sugar

splash of vinegar

Don't chuck the chicken carcass. Pick off any excess meat and save for a rainy day. Place the carcass in a pan and cover with water; add a peeled onion, carrot, garlic clove and some fresh herbs (parsley, thyme, bay). Bring to the boil, then turn down and simmer for 2 hours. Strain and use as stock.

HENRY'S TIPS

1 Heat the oven to 200°C. Season the bird all over. Smear the butter all over and inside. Put in a roasting tray. Halve the lemon and place inside the chicken with the garlic and thyme. Put in the hot oven to brown the skin: about 20 minutes. When coloured, cover with tin foil and turn the heat down to 170°C. The chicken will take about 45 minutes more to cook. To test, open the leg out, and if the joint pops out easily then it's ready. Don't be concerned if the meat looks slightly blushed. Leg meat is darker and will never look like white breast meat. Remove from the oven, and from the tray, and rest for 20 minutes.

2 To make a quick sauce, remove the lemon and garlic from the bird and place the tray over a gentle flame. Skim off any unwanted fat and scrape the crispers off the bottom. Squash the garlic and squeeze the lemon into the tray. Add the white wine, give it a quick boil, then stir in the flour. Pour in a few ladles of vegetable water or stock. Simmer for 5 minutes, add a pinch of sugar and splash of vinegar. Season and sieve into a jug.

MUSSEL CROQUETTES

• FEEDS 4 •

These are inspired by a Spanish tapas dish I had in Madrid a few years back. They work well as stand-alone morsels, but can also be served with a fresh tomato salad with some capers and basil and a vinegary dressing.

4 Desirée potatoes	50ml white wine	**FOR THE COATING:**
2 shallots	500g fresh mussels, well washed	2 eggs
2 garlic cloves	50ml double cream	50ml milk
30g butter	1 tbsp chopped parsley	30g flour
sprig of thyme	salt and pepper	100g breadcrumbs

1 Peel the potatoes and bring to a simmer in a pan of water.

2 Dice the shallot and slice the garlic. Heat a deep pan and gently melt half the butter. Add the shallot, garlic and thyme. Sweat for 3 minutes till soft but not coloured. Add the wine and bring to the boil, tip in the mussels and cover with a lid. Give the pan a shake and steam the mussels for 4 minutes, or until all are open.

3 Pour the mussels through a strainer, catching all the juices. Allow the mussels to cool before handling. Pour the strained mussel juice back into the pan and bring to the boil. Add the cream and reduce down to a nice consistency.

4 When the potatoes are cooked, drain and allow to steam dry over a low hob. Mash till smooth and beat in the mussel juice and cream mixture, add as much as you feel is right. You want quite a stiff mash, not a soup.

5 Pick the mussels out of their shells, roughly chop and fold gently through the mash with the remaining butter and the chopped parsley. Season to taste and leave to cool. When the mixture is cool enough to handle, roll into small log-shaped croquettes.

6 Whisk the eggs with the milk and a pinch of salt. Dust the croquettes in the flour and shake off the excess. Dip the croquettes into the egg mixture then roll in the breadcrumbs. Dip again into the egg and back through the crumbs. Firm up in the fridge.

7 Fry in hot oil (about 185°C) for 4 minutes until crispy and hot.

RHUBARB QUEEN OF PUDDINGS

FEEDS 4

This regal pudding, with its crispy meringue and soft pillowy base, has Sunday lunch written all over it. The classic recipe uses jam but I find it a bit sweet. Poaching the rhubarb gives a delicate, more subtle taste, as the fruit retains its natural flavour. See overleaf for the meringue part of the operation.

FOR THE BASE:	4 egg yolks	zest of 1 orange
50g butter	zest of 1–2 lemons	1 vanilla pod
600ml milk	**RHUBARB FILLING:**	1 small sprig of rosemary
150g fresh breadcrumbs	200g Yorkshire forced rhubarb	
25g sugar	50g caster sugar	

1 For the base, melt the butter into the milk in a saucepan and heat through. Stir in the breadcrumbs and sugar. Take off the heat, leave to cool and thicken a little, then stir in the egg yolks and lemon zest. Heat the oven to 180°C. Put the breadcrumb mixture into a greased baking dish (the one in which you will serve the pudding) and bake for 10–20 minutes until it looks set and slightly golden. Take out and set aside.

2 Meanwhile, top and tail the rhubarb and cut into 2cm batons. Place in a baking dish and sprinkle with the sugar and orange zest. Split the vanilla pod and scrape the seeds out of one half into the rhubarb. Save the other half for the meringue. Put the rosemary sprig on top, cover with foil and place in the oven at 180°C. Check every few minutes until the rhubarb is soft but not completely mushy. Remove from the oven and leave to cool. It is easier to handle the rhubarb when it's not piping hot. Quite a bit of juice will come out to make a lovely pink liquor. Taste it: it may need a touch of sugar if it's too tart, but don't over-sweeten as the rest of the pudding is sweet.

3 Spoon the poached rhubarb on top of the bread base, reserving some of the liquor if you have too much. Now to make the meringue topping.

ITALIAN MERINGUE

This stable meringue is less heavy than common meringue and doesn't need so long to cook because the sugar has already been cooked. It does require a temperature probe; if you don't have one, it can be a bit hit-or-miss.

75ml water

200g caster sugar

4 egg whites

In January and February, use Yorkshire forced rhubarb. In summer, use outdoor rhubarb. Any leftover liquor from the rhubarb can be used in cocktails as a flavour booster. Poached gooseberries in an elderflower syrup is equally delicious, though not as pretty. Or you can always make the classic version with jam instead.

HENRY'S TIPS

1 Place the water and sugar in a pan and bring to a soft boil, 121°C: this stabilises the sugar. Using an electric beater, beat the egg whites with the remaining vanilla seeds (from the rhubarb filling recipe) until they are firm. While the beaters are still running slowly, pour in the sugar syrup. Keep whisking until the meringue is cool and thick and glossy.

2 Place into a piping bag and artfully pipe on top of the rhubarb. You can go crazy at this stage as the meringue, if well made, will hold most shapes. Bake in the oven at 180°C for 20 minutes, till the peaks are brown and crispy and the rhubarb juice is bubbling through the edges.

CHAPATTIS PITTAS AND PIZZAS

FAST AND FURIOUS
DISCS OF JOY

Chapatti is the most brilliant bread in the world. It is certainly one of the most popular, and provides vital nutrition to millions every day. Honest, tasty, wholewheat goodness at its very best. When Henry's cooking up some spicy lamb, or we've dialled our friends at the Passage to India for a take-away, what to do to kill that longest half hour? Make chapatti, of course. This is ancient, timeless, unleavened bread.

I really love pitta breads. Not only are they great to eat, but during the cooking of them you can invite people to observe something dramatic happening, which is quite rare in the slow-is-best world of baking. If you have a very hot oven this bread is easy and blisteringly quick. No apologies, but you will be spoilt for packet pitta for evermore.

I recently met a New Yorker who declared he couldn't really be friends with someone who didn't like pizza. I know just what he means, but I also realise that way too many people haven't eaten a great pizza. Pizza is often sniffed at, perhaps because it fits into the cheap and fast camp of food options. Done simply and well, pizza can be a beautiful melted-cheesy-crispy disc of joy: *bellissimo*.

CHAPATTI

Wholemeal flour – it's the only notable ingredient you need. I've found chapatti to be a brilliant way to sample new wholemeal flours I've truffled out or that have come my way. Last trip I made to Pembrokeshire, I took in a tour of Y Felin water mill and bought a few bags of their Stoneground Biodynamic and Organic Spelt Flour. It tastes of a golden harvest in Laurie Lee's sweet and evocative valley.

1 Put two big double handfuls of wholemeal flour and a big pinch of salt into a large bowl, slowly add enough tepid water to bring it together, and mix with finger, fork or hook.* Knead the really soft dough for a good 15 minutes. Alternatively, blitz the lot in a food processor. The bran in wholemeal is hygroscopic and will keep on absorbing water for a long time, so keep working the dough until it's chewy and stretchy and beautifully soft. Add more water or flour until it feels good. Taste the dough for seasoning and add more salt if it's bland. Leave the dough to rest back in the bowl for a few moments while you dig out a heavy frying pan or flat griddle and get it heating up to smoking. Ensure your kitchen is ventilated and extractors are on. This is sure to set off the smoke alarm.

2 Divide the dough into 8 pieces. With a firm hand, shape them as round as you can. Then roll them out to about 6 inches (15cm) on a well-floured surface. Bake the chapatti one at a time. Drop the fibrous disc into the smokin' hot pan and, using a large pair of tongs, agitate it. When you can, give the chap a spin, don't let that sucker stick or burn. After 1 minute, flip it over and slightly scorch the underside, this should also take a minute at most. Risky, rewarding bit: if you're baking on gas, remove the pan from the heat and, using the long tongs, hold the chapatti directly over the flame. If your dough is stretchy enough, it'll blister and puff up a bit, or possibly dramatically inflate like a balloon. If gas isn't an option, a flash under the grill will work, or just a smidgeon longer in the pan. The hottest thing tonight ought to be the curry or the hostess, so take care not to set the kitchen and chapatti on fire. As a precaution, have a bucket of water to hand. This final, primal and manly touch is the authentic way to achieve the quintessential, bit charred, deliciously doughy, unctuousness that so dramatically and easily upstages the curry. Brush them with a little melted butter on one side and keep them warm, until the curry is ready. This is real bread, real fast and real good.

*If you really prefer to measure stuff out, use 250g wholemeal flour, 1/2 tsp salt and 170ml water.

TOM'S TIPS

MAN'S CURRY

━━ • FEEDS 2 MEN • ━━

I love a curry and a cool beer. It's so easy to make a delicious curry, and the smells of slow cooking lamb and spices are second to none. The best cut for a lamb curry is neck fillet, but this can be quite pricey, so I recommend diced shoulder. It is perfectly suited for slow cooking, and has that melt-in-the-mouth eating quality about it. Like all stews, it is always better the next day.

FOR THE PASTE:	2 onions, diced	vegetables of your choice, such as pepper and okra, chopped
4 garlic cloves	**FOR THE MEAT:**	
1 tbsp fresh ginger	500g diced lamb shoulder	400g tin of chopped tomatoes
pinch of cumin, coriander, garam masala, turmeric, cinnamon	a dollop of yogurt	200ml (half a tin) of coconut milk
	salt and pepper	bunch of fresh coriander
1 green and 1 red chilli, roughly chopped	oil for frying	
	30g ghee (clarified butter)	

1 First, in either a pestle and mortar or processor, blend all the paste ingredients except the onion. Take a few spoons out for the lamb, then add the onion and blend again.

2 Mix the diced lamb shoulder with the reserved paste, the yogurt and salt and pepper. Heat a frying pan, add a little oil and brown the meat on all sides. Remove and reserve.

3 Take a deep casserole and fry the onion paste in the ghee until golden. Careful, the chilli smell can be quite potent! Add the chopped vegetables and fry for a few minutes. Add the tinned tomatoes, then swill the can out with water and add to the pan as well. (My mother Polly taught me never to waste anything, even the residue in a tomato tin, and it also saves washing the tin for the recycling.) Bring to a gentle simmer, then add the lamb and the coconut milk. Turn the heat down and gently simmer for 2 hours: the lamb should be soft and giving but still juicy. Have a final season and spoon into bowls. Tear some coriander leaves over the top.

Diced breast of lamb is a cheaper option. It's fattier, like pork belly, but packed with flavour. If I was organised (which I'm not), I'd always make curry the day before I wanted to eat it. Serve with chapatti and a cool beer.

HENRY'S TIPS

QUICK FISH CURRY

— FEEDS 2 —

This may not be totally authentic, but it's quick to make and tastes good. It reminds me of curries I ate in Goa when I was travelling around India with my wife. On the first week back I made her this curry and she claimed it was the nicest she'd had.

oil for frying	1 onion, sliced	8 tiger prawns, raw and peeled
3 garlic cloves, grated	1 red pepper, sliced	fresh coriander leaves, to serve
1 knob of fresh ginger, peeled and grated	400g tin of chopped tomatoes	
	200ml (half a tin) of coconut milk	
1 green chilli, diced	1 lemon	
1 pinch each of spices: cumin, coriander, turmeric, ginger, curry leaves, cinnamon bark, cardamom (plus extra for the fish)	sugar, salt and pepper	
	200g diced white fish, bream or red mullet	
	4 scallops	

1 Heat a large pan, add a tablespoon of oil and quickly fry the garlic, ginger and chilli. Add the spices and fry for 1–2 minutes. Add the onion and cook until soft. Stir in the red pepper and tomatoes. Cook down for 5 minutes, then pour in the coconut milk and simmer for 15 minutes.

2 Taste the curry: it may need a squeeze of lemon and a pinch of sugar. Season with salt and pepper.

3 Sprinkle the fish, scallops and prawns with a pinch or two of spice, and season. Heat a frying pan with a little oil and brown the fish off quickly and carefully: don't shake it around but move it as little as possible. Add to the curry and cook until just done: about 2 minutes. Serve with coriander leaves.

HENRY'S TIPS

Curry leaves can be hard to find, but they make all the difference. If you see them, buy lots, then dry the spare ones out and they will keep for a couple of months. Fish curry is delicious with chapatti and basmati rice.

TANDOORI-STYLE CHICKEN CHAPATTI WRAP

MAKES 4

An Indian-style wrap, so good you will want another. Chapattis are as good at carrying a filling as they are at mopping up curry sauce. If you have time, marinate the chicken overnight.

4 boneless chicken legs, skin off (or breast if you must)	2 garlic cloves, crushed	about 2 tsp in total of mixed spices: cumin, coriander, chilli powder, paprika, cardamom, clove
	1 tsp freshly grated ginger	
4 warm chapattis	1 lemon juice	
FOR THE MARINADE:	1 tsp oil	salt and pepper
4 tbsp yogurt		

1 Mix all the marinade ingredients together, rub all over the chicken and leave for a few hours or overnight.

2 Gently fry the chicken in a pan or under the grill for about 15–20 minutes. Remove and, while still warm, cut into slices. Wrap in warm chapattis.

HENRY'S TIPS

Serve with yogurt sauce (see page 116) and slaw (page 118). I like to add some sliced green chillies to give it some kick, and some torn fresh coriander. Cold beer seems to hit the nail as well. Keep the chapattis warm in a tea towel so they fold and roll easily.

PITTA BREAD

AS MANY AS YOU WANT

Pitta breads once saved my life . . . I agreed to give a breadmaking demonstration for the Minchinhampton Church ladies group, and there was such an enthusiastic take-up that I ended up with more people than I could easily fit in the bakery. I couldn't back out. I decided to make pitta, because I could have the dough ready and waiting to be rolled out and baked. I asked the participants to be at the bakery at 7.30 p.m. By 7.35 I was still waiting: it was a no-show. I couldn't figure it out. They'd been so keen. Then I looked out of the window and saw them. Coming across the road were thirty women of a certain age, all wearing aprons and brandishing rolling pins. I was terrified! Thankfully the pitta breads worked their impressive magic on the formidable group.

1 Before you start on the dough, heat the oven up to maximum – at least 230°C – with the baking stone in place. If you haven't got a baking stone, use a baking tray.

2 Using the white dough after its first rise (see page 50), weigh out the number of pittas you need at 100g each. Shape each piece into a ball and, on a well-floured work surface, roll out the pittas with a rolling pin in one direction only, keeping both sides well dusted with flour so it doesn't stick. Keep on pinning until the pitta is the length of your arm, from knuckle to elbow.

3 Once you've got it, grab oven gloves, pull out the rack bearing the baking stone, lie the pitta on top, slide it back and shut the door. After 30 seconds or so, the thin cool dough on the baking hot stone will start to blister, and all things being favourable a great airship of dough will alarmingly balloon up. In only a minute (before it takes on too much colour), your pitta is baked. Take great care when removing it not to burn yourself as the pitta exhales steam. Repeated in this fashion, a cairn of dough pockets of joy will soon be ready for filling and eating.

Starting out, only about three-quarters of my pittas opened evenly, so reckon on making some extra. Imperfect ones are great for dips. The more evenly you pin them out, the better chance they'll open fully. The hotter your baking stone, the greater the possibility of perfect pittas too. A wood-fired oven at 300°C or more would be ace.

TOM'S TIPS

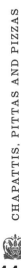

EIGHT-HOUR SMOKY PULLED PORK SHOULDER

━━━ FEEDS 15 ━━━

Very few people, on seeing unctuous steaming-hot smoky pork, can resist the temptation to sneak a little piece. With crackling to die for and the softest pork ever, all you will want to do is pile it into a hot pitta, heap up the pickles and devour. This dish is best made for a crowd as cooking small quantities doesn't quite work. I use the descending heat of our wood-fired oven because it welcomes you in the morning with the best smell ever. In a domestic oven, you can easily achieve the same result by turning the oven down low and cooking slowly through the day, ready for the evening.

1 hand of pork from the shoulder	100ml olive oil	250ml bottle of beer
30g smoked paprika	100ml Worcestershire sauce	salt and pepper
1 bulb of garlic, smashed	1 bunch of thyme	freshly made hot pittas, to serve

1 Put all the ingredients except the pork in a large bowl and give it a good mix, then massage over the pork, getting into all the nooks and crannies. The pork can be cooked straight away, but will benefit from marinating in the fridge overnight.

2 Heat the oven to 200°C. Put the pork in a large tin and roast in the hot oven for 20–30 minutes until the skin is starting to crackle. When you're happy with the crackling, turn the heat down to 140°C and cover with foil but don't seal the edges. The pork will take about 8 hours: the longer the better. You will know when it is done because the meat will pull easily off the bone.

HENRY'S TIPS

To take your pulled pork to the next level, cold-smoke it. First, brine it. Boil 3 litres of water in a stockpot with 1kg salt, 250g sugar and some peppercorns. Allow to cool, then submerge the shoulder and make space in the fridge. Brine for 3 days, then cold-smoke in your smoker (page 185) for 2 days.

CHAPATTIS, PITTAS AND PIZZAS

114

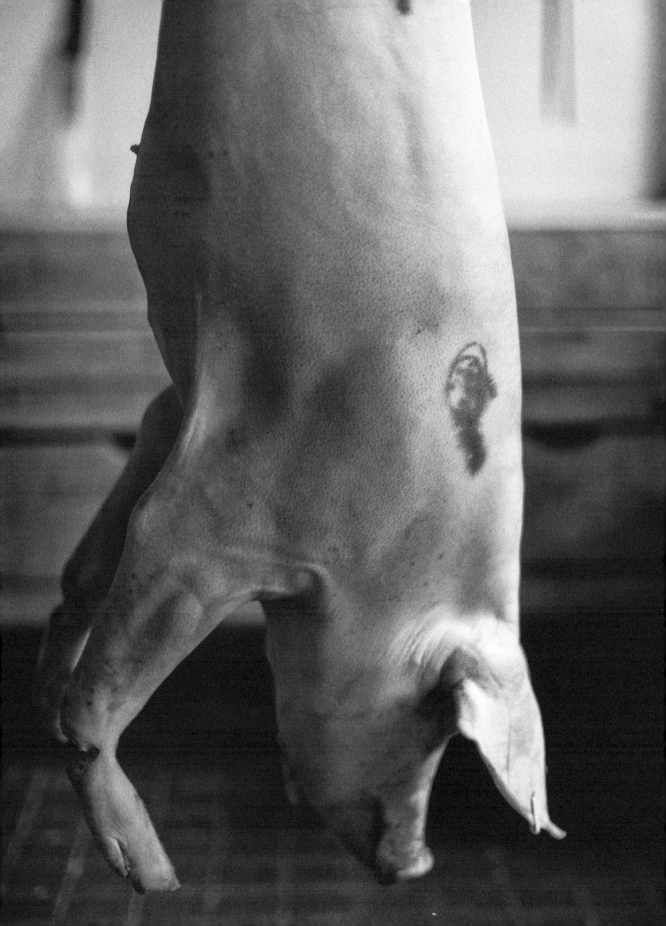

SLOW ROAST LAMB SHOULDER WITH GARLIC YOGURT

• FEEDS 8 TO 10 •

Lamb shoulder, slow-roasted for five hours in the descending heat of a wood-fired oven, so tender that the meat just falls off the bone, piled into hot pittas with a garlicky yogurt sauce, what could be better? A perfect dish for a small crowd.

1 lamb shoulder on the bone	salad leaves and freshly made hot pittas, to serve	bunch of mint
3 garlic cloves		500g yogurt
20ml olive oil	**FOR THE GARLIC YOGURT:**	
salt and pepper	1 small cucumber	
bunch of rosemary	2 or 3 garlic cloves	

1 Peel and chop the garlic, place into a pestle and mortar with the oil, salt and pepper and rosemary. Bash it around till you have a nice paste. Rub this all over the lamb, getting into all the nooks and crannies. Leave for a few hours if you have time.

2 Heat the oven to 200°C. Put the lamb in an oven tray and let it brown in the hot oven, then cover with foil, reduce the heat to 140°C and let the oven to do its magic for the next 5 hours or so. When the meat slides off the bones with ease, take it out and rest for 30 minutes.

3 Halve the cucumber and spoon out the seeds. Grate on a coarse setting and sprinkle with salt, which will draw out the moisture. After 5 minutes, give it a quick wash and squeeze the excess liquid out. Finely dice the garlic and

the mint leaves, stir into the yogurt with the cucumber. Taste and adjust the seasoning. It will taste better after 2 hours and will keep for a few days in the fridge, but be warned the garlic will get stronger and stronger.

4 Fill the pittas with some leaves, big chunks of lamb and spoon over some garlic yogurt.

Really good with raw crunchy beetroot and red cabbage slaw (see overleaf). Lamb shoulder off the bone is fine for this dish, but cooks in half the time.

HENRY'S TIPS

BEETROOT AND RED CABBAGE SLAW FOR LAMB PITTAS

• FEEDS 8 •

This vibrant slaw is perfect with the lamb pittas. It also works well with other fatty meats such as pork belly or shoulder, or pot-roast beef brisket.

1 red cabbage	1 lemon, halved	small bunch tarragon or parsley, leaves finely chopped
3 beetroot	salt and pepper	
1 red onion	50ml extra virgin olive oil	

1 Using a mandolin or a very sharp knife, slice the red cabbage as thinly as possible. Grate the beetroot into a bowl and finely dice the red onion. Mix the vegetables together. Squeeze the lemon over and season with salt and pepper. It is best left for 30 minutes, as the lemon and salt will slightly soften the cabbage. Add the olive oil and stir in the chopped herbs.

If you want to make it creamy, a few dollops of crème fraîche is rather good, though you don't need it for the lamb pittas. A chopped green chilli stirred through adds a big hit in small spaces. If you want to be more classic, make a slaw from white cabbage, onion and carrot instead.

HENRY'S TIPS

ESTD 1920

PIZZA BASES

MAKES 8 LARGE BASES

In my bakery/café in Nailsworth, we might only do a couple of pizzas on a midweek lunchtime, but I needed them on the menu, so I devised a way of making a big batch, lightly baking them, then piling them up in the freezer until they're needed. Being really thin, the pizza bases defrost by the time the toppings are added, and because they are already lightly baked, they're really easy to get into the oven without using a peel. I always keep some in the freezer at home and I find they inspire the best quick meals. I came up with this recipe for pizza bases at Fforests summer bakery on the bank of the river Teifi in Cardigan town. The local water mill, Y Felin, mills a delicious spelt flour, which I incorporated into the recipe for a sweet nuttiness.

750g strong white flour	20g sea salt	570ml warm water
250g wholemeal flour, such as spelt	10g dried yeast (or 20g fresh yeast if you can get it)	80ml olive oil (nothing fancy for baking with)

1 Weigh all the ingredients into a mixing bowl and mix well until you have a very soft and stretchy dough. This should take about 15 minutes by hand, and 12 minutes if done in a mixer. It's really important not to shirk on the kneading; to get an elastic, super-stretchy dough that is robust and will give you great pizzas you really need to put the effort in at this stage.

2 Put the dough back into the mixing bowl, cover and leave in a warm place to rest for an hour.

3 Tip the dough onto a clean flat work surface and divide into eight pieces of 200g each. Then make a claw from your hand and, using a circular action and a bit of palm pressure, mould the pizzas into tight round rolls.

4 Slosh a good glug of olive oil into a big roasting tin and roll the bases around in it, coating each dough ball with oil (this will stop them proving into each other, and give the pizza base a lush crust). Cover and leave in a warm place to rise for half an hour or so.

5 Meanwhile, fire the oven up as hot as it will go with a baking stone in place. Anything above 230°C will work but 350–400°C in a wood-fired oven is best.

TOM'S TIPS

No two flours are the same. If, during the mixing and kneading stage, you feel the dough is too slack and wet, then add a small amount of additional flour; if it's too tight and dry, add a little more water.

6 Now to make your pizzas round-ish. I love throwing pizza bases. It's permissible showing off when you're making food for people, and once you have it licked it's quicker too. It all starts by taking an oiled dough piece and gently stretching it out whilst rotating, passing the rim from one hand to the other, so the dough, hanging down, takes on a side-plate form. Now, get the oily dough hanging over your knuckles. Hold it in front of your face and, with an explosive jerk and flick of the wrist, send the doughy disc towards the ceiling, spinning as it goes. The weight in the rim and centrifugal force will, after a dozen throws, reward you with an awesome pizza base. Stop if holes start to open (just pinch them shut). Then blind-bake the base directly on the baking/pizza stone for just a couple of minutes. Take it out once there is the slightest hint of colour. Time it so that the next base is thrown and ready once the previous base has been blind-baked.

7 Once they are all made, allow the oven to build up heat and start topping and making pizzas. With a blind-baked base you can finish the pizzas under a grill. Any unused bases can be frozen until you need them. Just place a small square of baking parchment between each one so they don't freeze together.

ROLLING PIN ALTERNATIVE:

With plenty of semolina flour on the table, by using a rolling pin and rotating the pizza base as you go, a beautifully flat and even base with a nice bit of crunch can be easily achieved. Top and bake in a very hot oven in the traditional way.

TOM'S TIPS

The oven temperature might drop after baking a few, with the door being frequently opened; give it time to come back up to temperature so your bases are consistently crisp. I don't worry about small blisters in the base when they are baking, but anything bigger than a garlic bulb I'd pop.

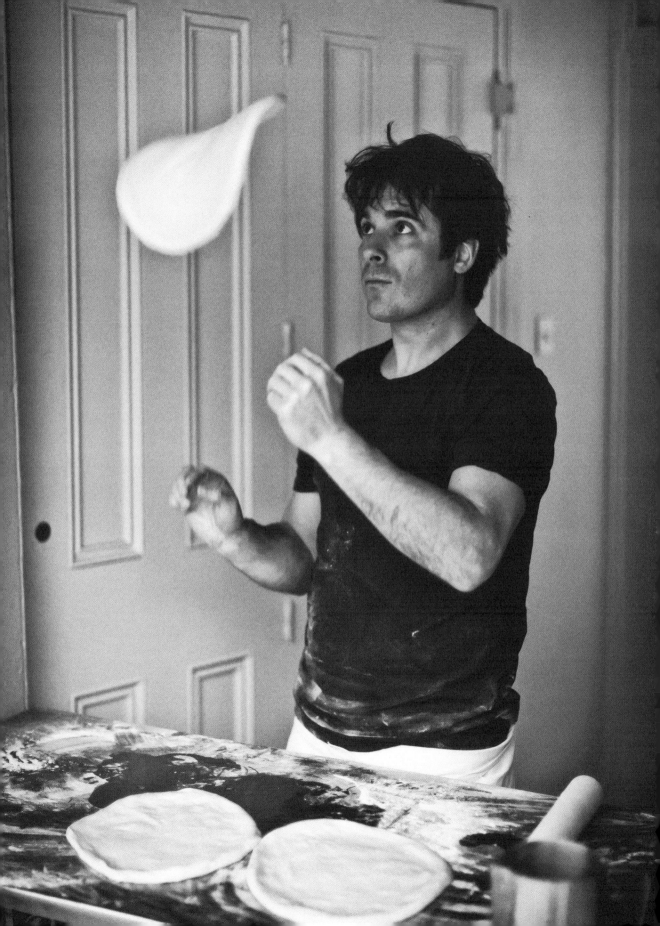

PIZZAS

FEEDS 1 HUNGRY PERSON

Everyone has their preference when it comes to pizza. Here are a few of our favourites. These recipes use the part-baked pizza bases, which have the added advantage of being easier to lift. If you are using a freshly made base (a 200g ball of dough rolled as thin as you dare), then a little skill is needed to get it into the oven. Use a bread peel that is well floured, quickly flick the peel under the pizza base, and, when it is on, quickly flick it onto the baking stone. This can cause some pizza casualties until you've got the hang of it. The oven needs to be hotter than hot; a wood-fired oven is the best. If not, make sure you use a baking stone as this is the only way to get a crispy bottom.

BASIC TOMATO SAUCE

People often overcomplicate a tomato sauce for a pizza. This one is simple and good.

2 garlic cloves
400g tin of tomatoes
1 tsp dried oregano
2 tbsp extra virgin olive oil
salt and pepper

Grate the garlic into a blender and add the other ingredients. Whizz together briefly till you have a smoothish sauce. This tomato sauce will keep well for 1 week.

MARGHERITA

The classic: tomato and cheese. Spread a thin layer of tomato sauce almost to the edges of the pizza base. It's important not to put too much on a pizza; it's definitely a case of less is more. Take the finest mozzarella (buffalo is my preference), drain it from its water womb, tear bits off and dot over the pizza. Bake it in a hot oven until the topping is melted and brown and the base is crisp. Remove, tear over some fresh basil and drizzle with chilli oil if you're feeling authentic.

To make your own chilli oil, take a bottle of extra virgin oil, down to its last quarter. Poke down the top three hot red chillies that have been scored slightly to allow the flavour to infuse quicker. Leave to infuse for at least a month or two. The result is perfect and gets better over time.

HENRY'S TIPS

OLIVE, ANCHOVY AND CAPERS

This is my personal favourite. I love anything pickled and salty, so the mixture of vinegary olives, salty anchovies and pungent capers is heaven. Much the same as the margherita, spread a little sauce and dot some mozzarella around. Add a few pitted black olives and fillets of anchovy and a scattering of capers. Fire in the oven until crisp and bubbling, then drizzle with some extra virgin olive oil and grind a few twists of black pepper over.

GARLIC, ROAST BEEF AND ROCKET

This pizza shows it's not all about cheese and tomato. Rub the base with a garlic clove that has been sprinkled with salt and left for 5 minutes. This draws out the garlic juice. You'll get just a hint of garlic, rather than a full-on whack. Drizzle with extra virgin olive oil and bake until hot and crispy. Remove and place a few strips of thinly sliced rare roast beef (leftovers from Sunday's dinner work well), and top with a small bunch of well-dressed rocket leaves. A few shavings of Parmesan are also nice, as is a dribble of truffle oil.

LAMB AND SAGE PIZZA

Bianca (pizza without tomato) is Tom's current favourite. In this one, the lamb is in small meat balls spiked with lemon zest. You can either use lamb sausages and mix in the lemon zest, or make your own using lamb mince with some crushed garlic, salt and pepper and an egg to bind together. Roll into little walnut-sized balls and set aside. Spread some double cream over the pizza base. Place the lamb balls around. Not too many per base: say, 8. Finely chop some sage leaves and sprinkle over. Season with salt and pepper and bake for up to 5 minutes until crisp and golden. It may sound like an odd combination but it really is delicious and worth a try.

ASH-BAKED FLATBREADS WITH RAZOR CLAMS

MAKES ABOUT 20

This is from Antony Smith of the Hobbs House Bistro. As Ant has put more and more fire-related things on the Bistro menu, and his reputation has fanned out, so the call of the wild has got stronger for me, and I find myself often out in the sticks with my kids building fires to cook stuff on. This flatbread method served me well while baking in the woods for the Do Lectures.

FOR THE DOUGH:
Use the pizza dough from page 121; if you like, make it entirely with strong white flour, 1kg in total

FOR THE FIRE:
bed of hot embers (about 20–30 minutes after the flames have died down)

bucket of cold ash

a pair of baker's hands, or, if you don't have these, tongs

FOR THE CLAMS:
3 large, diver-caught razor clams per person

olive oil

sea salt

CHILLI DRESSING
4 large, mild, deseeded red chillies

handful of parsley leaves

2 garlic cloves

olive oil

1 Once the dough has had its first rise, shape into balls around 60–80g each (the size of an apple). Allow to prove again, then roll out until a bit thicker than a pound coin.

2 Scatter the cold ash over the embers. Place a flatbread on the embers. They should take around a minute each side. You are looking for light, puffed-up breads with patches of charred dough. Dust off any excess ash, check for hot rocks stuck in the dough, and eat hot.

3 Cook the clams on the embers. Once they open, carefully brush them with olive oil. Allow them to sizzle for a minute. Gingerly remove them from the fire (their shells will now be brittle and can break). Sprinkle the flesh with good sea salt and eat with the hot bread.

4 For the chilli dressing, finely chop the chillies, parsley and garlic. Add enough oil to bring it together into a consistency you like. Season, put in a jar and take with you into the wilds. Use to dress the hot clams.

If you're in the sticks, an unopened can of beer or bottle of wine makes a reasonable rolling pin, or just flatten the breads out in your hand.

TOM'S TIPS

SOURDOUGH AND SODA BREAD

MAJESTIC SOURDOUGH
AND SUPERFAST SODA

The sourdough, a simple flour-and-water fermentation, is an ancient breadmaking technique which is now making the most contemporary of loaves. If we are pursuing the idea that the more you put into something, the more you get out of it, then sourdough rewards massively. You have to look after your sourdough culture and keep it going. And it's got a story, depending on where you got it from. I share my sourdough with people who come on my breadmaking courses, and in this way the Hobbs House 'Monster' has found its way into bakeries and kitchens all over the country. An aspect of sourdough that is both wondrous and troubling is its exponential growth potential. The more you feed it, the bigger it becomes, and the more loaves you can rise. With a bit of time, we could rise all the world's loaves this way.

My monkey-proof recipe for spelt soda bread ticks all the boxes, especially if one of those boxes is break-neck-speed-bread. This is a traditional Irish loaf, risen with bicarbonate of soda. You can easily be eating this loaf within forty-five minutes of any baking notion. I make mine with spelt flour, whose many qualities include a reputation for being easily digested, which is something to bear in mind with such a fast-risen loaf as this. Once mastered, soda bread can be adapted in many ways, with fruit, treacle, honey, nuts, seeds, herbs, cheese. You could even make your own butter, giving you buttermilk to go into the soda bread before baking, with the butter to melt into a fresh hot slice afterwards.

SOURDOUGH LOAF

MAKES 1 LARGE LOAF

An almighty, kingly loaf, risen very slowly with a sourdough culture. This keeps very well, and tastes and looks fantastic. A great loaf with any meal and a fat slice will make wonderfully regal toast. Sourdough is the king of breads.

FEEDING THE SOURDOUGH	10g sea salt	Proving basket
225g sourdough in jar (see page 136)	230ml warm water	Oven: 230°C at baking time
	KIT:	Baking stone
75g warm water	Set of scales, preferably digital	Sharp knife
75g wholemeal flour	Large mixing bowl or mixer with dough hook	Water sprayer
MAKING THE LOAF:		Oven gloves
460g strong white flour	Scraper	
300g sourdough culture	Cling film or a shower cap	

1 Feed the sourdough 12 hours before you start making your loaf. Take the jar containing 225g sourdough out of the fridge and add 75g warm water and 75g wholemeal flour and give it a stir. If you are following the plan on page 136, you will have already done this stage and can go straight into making the bread.

2 Weigh all the ingredients into the mixing bowl. Using the scraper, mix them all together to form a rough wet dough. Turn it onto the work surface and knead, putting your body weight behind the effort. Stretch and work the dough vigorously for 15 minutes. Once a beautifully soft and stretchy dough has formed, put it back into the mixing bowl, cover with cling film (or a shower cap) and leave in a warm place to relax and rise for 3–4 hours.

3 Now feed your sourdough for next time. You should have 75g left in the jar. Add to it 75g cool water and 75g wholemeal flour, stir and put in the fridge where it'll keep for several weeks.

4 With a light dusting of flour on the work surface, empty the dough out of the bowl and mould the dough into a loaf shape. Dust the proving basket generously with flour and place the moulded dough piece, seam side up, in the basket and leave it covered with cling film (or shower cap) overnight to double in size, for about 12 hours.

5 Heat the oven and baking stone to 230°C and gently tease the dough onto the baking stone. Give it your signature cut, spray it with a few spritzes from your water sprayer and bake for half an hour until beautifully golden and it makes a hollow sound when tapped on the bottom.

STARTING A
SOURDOUGH CULTURE

Mother, monster, bigga, whatever you call it, this is how to start your own delicious wild-yeast bread-rising culture, and establish a brilliant, shareable tradition.

Find a suitable container to house your sourdough. A Kilner jar is good.

Clean it well and weigh it while it's empty, noting the weight on an address tag or label. (This saves you having to empty it out to know how much you have left – it'll be worth it later.)

Weigh 75g organic wholemeal or dark rye or wholemeal spelt flour into the jar (any of these will work well), then weigh in 75g/ml warm water. Stir.

Leave your jar in a prominent and warm place (its second home) in your kitchen, with the lid sealed.

Each day for a week, repeat the feeding process (75g flour and 75g water, as before), stirring vigorously with a clean finger or a fork to remove all floury lumps.

After about 5 days you'll notice bubbles in the dough. Like the first windy smile of a baby, you know that soon enough it'll be laughing and telling jokes, and you're on your way to the most rewarding kind of baking. You can use the culture at this stage, but it will be slow and weak.

After the first week, you can start to keep the culture in the fridge (its first home), only removing it a day or so before use, to feed it back into full bubbly liveliness (75g flour and 75g water, as before). After a month, the dough will have matured and you'll be getting great flavour and rising performance from it.

It's quite laughable just how simple it can be to keep your sourdough in peak condition for really tasty loaves, if you feed it occasionally and mostly keep it in the fridge.

Surplus sourdough can be used to flavour all manner of buns, cakes and pancakes.

If the sourdough is not performing well enough, try taking it out of the fridge a day before you want to use it, and giving it an extra feed. Remember that, as a living culture, it needs to be fed if it's not hibernating in the fridge (where it can survive for several months). It likes to be warm and aerated (stirred/whisked) occasionally.

If it dies ('de-natures' – you'll know because it will smell disgusting), bin it and start again.

I'm custodian of our family sourdough that's been rising award-winning loaves at Hobbs House Bakery for over 55 years. With a bit of good husbandry and some forward planning, yours could live just as long, or longer.

FEEDING A SOURDOUGH CULTURE

Your sourdough is alive. If you don't look after it, it will die. Keeping the sourdough alive couldn't be simpler, if you mostly keep it in the fridge and feed it occasionally.

The sourdough bread recipe on page 132 requires 300g of sourdough.

Know the weight of your container so you can weigh the sourdough without creating washing up.

Ideally, you should always retain at least a quarter of your sourdough so you don't dilute its flavour and performance.

Feed your sourdough more if you wish to bake more loaves or create more sourdough culture to share. This will momentarily dilute the flavour.

Sourdough culture often separates after a day or two. Just stir the grey water back in when you feed it.

Keep a small quantity of sourdough frozen in case of emergency, and if necessary defrost and follow the weekly plan.

Now you have a sourdough, you can name it. I found the anthropomorphising of my sourdough culture particularly helpful when I was about to leave it in the custody of an apprentice ('Baldrick'). The culture was going through a particularly virile stage and had built up a head of steam when – *KABOOOM!* – it blew its lid off, taking out a bulb in the overhead ultraviolet insectocutor. It had earned its moniker, the 'Monster' (it's alive, it'll bite), and I was able to make it clear to Baldrick that, like the sourdough, I'd explode and put his lights out if he didn't look after it and feed it while I was away.

WEEKLY PLAN

Once you've established your sourdough, follow this plan to have a loaf of freshly baked bread every Saturday morning. Should you want to bake more loaves, just multiply the recipe in anticipation of your bake.

1. Start with 75g of sourdough remaining, having just mixed a batch of dough.

2. Feed the culture 75g flour and 75g cold water (it will now weigh 225g), and refrigerate.

3. On Friday morning, remove the sourdough from the fridge and feed it again with 75g flour and 75g warm water. It'll now weigh 375g, the target weight for this process (300g for the recipe and 75g to keep). Leave it somewhere warm.

4. On Friday evening, weigh and mix the sourdough following the instructions on the sourdough loaf recipe page (see page 132: you can skip the feeding stage described there, since you've already done it). You will have 75g sourdough remaining.

5. Return to step 1.

Should your sourdough culture be lacklustre and sluggish, or if you're using it for the first time after an extended hibernation in the fridge, start the weekly revival process a day early and give an additional feed.

CHEESE TOASTIE

· FEEDS 1 ·

This recipe is based on Todd's Toasties from Trethowan's Dairy, featured in my programme *In Search of the Perfect Loaf*. Quite possibly the finest bread snack known to man. They are quick and easy to make, and the aroma is haunting.

2 fairly thin slices of sourdough
100g mature Cheddar, grated

50g combined onion and leek, finely chopped

1 Sandwich the grated Cheddar, onion and leek evenly between the slices of sourdough and place in a heated, oiled toastie machine for several minutes, until the cheese has melted into the bread and formed the most amazing golden crust.

2 Eat straight away. Warning: hot cheese on chin, danger of burnt mouth due to irresistible aroma.

TOM'S TIPS

Use 5-day-old sourdough bread for a better, firmer toastie, and the best Cheddar you can find. Cut the loaf at an angle to achieve a larger slice to hold even more of the cheese. In our bakery we use Keen's unpasteurised Cheddar, a fellow fifth-generation artisan family, making the tastiest, earthiest cheese around.

WOODCOCK WITH LIVER CROUTE

— FEEDS 2 —

If you manage to shoot a woodcock you deserve a pat on the back. If you're like us mere mortals, source one from your local butchery. Roasted whole till just pink, resting on a sourdough croute, with the livers quickly fried in the pan juices and a slug of Madeira then spread on the toast. Not to mention splitting the skull open to lap up the brains. This may not appeal to those of a weak disposition but I love it. I cooked this one particularly hung-over Saturday morning with my mate Ant (who I have worked with for years). The smell of rich game wafted through the house and by the time I had demolished this tiny but mighty bird I was feeling quite dandy and ready to approach the world again.

2 woodcocks, plucked but not drawn	15ml oil	30ml Madeira
	30g butter	small bunch of watercress
salt and pepper	2 slices of sourdough	

1 Heat the oven to 200°C. Season the woodcocks inside and out. Heat a frying pan and add the oil. Gently brown the woodcocks. When coloured, add half the butter and baste the woodcocks to give them a nice shine.

2 Place the sourdough slices on an oven tray. Balance the woodcocks upright on top and roast for 8 minutes. Give the breasts a quick squeeze to see if they are done. By this point, the sourdough will be nice and crispy on the bottom.

3 Remove the woodcocks and their croutes. Scoop the liver and insides out of the birds' cavities. Discard any bits that look unpleasant to your eyes – though all of the bird is edible. Pour the baking tray juices into the frying pan, add the remaining butter, and when foaming add the liver, *et al*. Quickly fry for 2 minutes, then pour in the Madeira and reduce, season to taste and spread the livers on the sourdough croutes. Serve with some dressed watercress with the woodcock sitting proudly on top.

SOURDOUGH AND SODA BREAD

DEVILLED LAMB'S KIDNEYS

• FEEDS 2 •

Some say this is good for breakfast, but that's a bit like drinking before 11 a.m.;
I like kidneys a little later in the day when I've warmed my stomach up a tad.

2 slices of sourdough	20g flour	50ml dark stock, lamb or beef
4 fresh lamb's kidneys, split, sinew removed	1 tbsp oil	knob of cold butter
pinch of cayenne	salt and pepper	1 tsp finely chopped parsley
1 tsp mustard powder	10ml Worcestershire sauce	
	20ml dry sherry	

1 Mix the cayenne, mustard powder and flour. Dust the lamb's kidneys in and shake off. Heat a small frying pan and heat the oil. Season the kidneys and place, smooth side down, into the pan and fry for 2 minutes, then turn the kidneys over and gently fry for a few more minutes. We want a kidney that is just slightly pink.

2 Transfer the kidneys from the pan to a warm plate and rest. Pop the toast in the toaster. With the pan still on, pour in the Worcestershire sauce and sherry. Boil away and scrape up the pan crispers on the bottom. When reduced by two-thirds, add the stock and boil again. Now taste the sauce: it should be hot, slightly acidic and meaty. When the sauce is of a pleasant consistency, add the cold butter and parsley. Shake the pan so the butter emulsifies with the sauce to give it a glossy finish and to soften any harsh offaly flavours and counter the acidity.

3 When happy with the sauce, place the kidneys on the toast and coat with the devilled sauce. Serve to someone you love.

SOURDOUGH AND SODA BREAD

140

BROWN CRAB ON TOAST

FEEDS 2 OR 4

This might be my favourite thing on toast. You can't beat a crab sandwich, but a piece of toasted sourdough with a huge pile of seasoned crab meat is pure indulgence. Buy the best brown crab meat you can find. Portland shellfish is, in my opinion, the finest. This dish always reminds me of a lush day spent with Jess in Port Isaac in Cornwall one summer. We bought a pot of crab and a loaf. We had been camping so I had a few condiments up my sleeve. I knocked up this dish and we ate it sitting on the harbour wall with a bottle of chilled prosecco. I'm dreaming of that place as I write.

4 slices of sourdough	juice of ½ lemon	
250g freshly picked brown crab meat	1 tbsp Worcestershire sauce	
	pinch of cayenne	
2 tbsp mayonnaise (for home-made, see page 90)	1 tsp finely chopped tarragon	
	salt and pepper	

1 Add all the ingredients bar the sourdough to a mixing bowl, and stir together. Taste the crab: it should be rich and creamy. The mayonnaise helps this with a background warming kick, while the lemon and tarragon give it that fresh tang to lift it off.

2 Toast the sourdough and pile the crab on top. I like to serve it with some dressed leaves and a lemon wedge.

GENTLEMAN'S RELISH WITH SCRAMBLED EGG

— FEEDS 2 —

I was taught a similar dish while at college. I don't remember the exact recipe, but I do recall the scrambled egg being set into a mould so it stood up like Chinese rice. These days, I'm not so fussed about shape, but the combination of hot toast with a thin layer of anchovy spread and buttery eggs is a good one in my eyes.

2 slices of sourdough	5 free-range eggs	salt and pepper
30g butter	30ml milk	1 tsp Gentleman's relish

1 Gently heat a non-stick pan and melt the butter. Break the eggs in, add the milk and mix together.

2 As the egg starts to heat, stir the mixture gently. If, like me, you like big folds of egg, don't beat it too roughly as the egg coagulates.

3 Just before the mixture thickens too much, season with salt and pepper and take off the heat. Remember that the egg will continue to cook off the heat, so remove the egg just before it is done to your liking.

4 Drop the sourdough into the toaster. Spread a thin layer of Gentleman's relish on the toast and pile the scrambled egg on top. Serve immediately with a black coffee and a pot of Dijon.

> **HENRY'S TIPS**
>
> Don't season the egg until the last minute, because the salt breaks down the protein (albumen) and causes the egg to lose its structure, resulting in runny eggs.

WILD MUSHROOM AND FRIED DUCK EGG

• FEEDS 2 •

Great as a quick lunch dish. Try to use mushrooms in season. If hard to find, flat mushrooms are still delicious. I love Scottish girolles when in season. Duck eggs have a larger, richer yolk than hen's but can be difficult to find.

2 slices of sourdough	200g wild mushrooms, cleaned	2 duck eggs
20g butter	salt and pepper	
1 garlic clove, crushed	10g finely chopped parsley	

1 Heat a frying pan and add half the butter and the garlic. As it starts to foam, add the mushrooms and toss. Fry for a few minutes, then season and toss with parsley. When you add salt to mushrooms the water is drawn out, so it's better to colour them before they go soggy.

2 Heat another small frying pan and add the remaining butter and a splash of oil. Fry the eggs gently so they are slightly crispy on the edges but not too coloured on their butts. In my view it's not a fried egg unless you fry it, so crispy edges are a must. Toast the sourdough and pile each slice with the mushrooms and top with a fried egg.

HENRY'S TIPS

I recommend a spoon of Dijon to finish it off, but then I do have rather a taste for the stuff.

LAMB SWEETBREADS, CAPERS AND PARSLEY

• FEEDS 2 •

From the thymus gland, these creamy organs are a real treat. If cooked properly, they are absolute heaven. They work well in salads and as a garnish to meatier dishes, but I like them on toast. Your local butcher should be able to get sweetbreads for you. They are best from new-season lamb, from spring to summer.

2 slices of sourdough	salt and pepper	pinch of sugar
8 sweetbreads	1 tbsp capers	small knob of butter
1 tbsp vegetable oil	splash of sherry vinegar	1 tbsp chopped parsley

1 Bring a large pan of water to the boil. Have a bowl of cold water ready, with ice cubes in if possible. Drop the sweetbreads into the boiling water for 10 seconds, remove and plunge into the ice water. This cooks the outside membrane and makes it easier to remove. If you don't do this, sweetbreads can be a little chewy. Using a small knife, peel off the thin outside skin. Not all will come off, but most will. Drain and set aside.

2 Heat a frying pan and add the oil. Season the sweetbreads and put in the pan. Fry on each side for 2 minutes. I like mine barely medium.

3 When they are looking nicely browned, add the capers, vinegar and sugar. This gives the sweetbreads a sweet and sour kick, which is really good with offal. Drop the sourdough into the toaster to toast.

4 Add the butter to the pan and toss in the parsley. Place on top of the toast and enjoy.

HERRING ROES ON TOAST

━━━━ FEEDS 2 ━━━━

This dish is one of three things I remember my grandfather cooking, along with his special breakfast recipe and mint sauce. Herring roes are the sperm sacs of male herrings; don't let this deter you, they are absolutely delicious and surprisingly cheap as well.

2 slices of sourdough	1 tsp capers	salt and pepper
20g butter	1 squeeze of lemon	
6 herring roes	pinch of chopped parsley	

1 So quick to make, I would put the toast on first.

2 Heat a frying pan and add half the butter. When foaming, tip in the roes. Brown off for 2 minutes. Carefully turn and add the capers. After 2 minutes, add the rest of the butter and let it foam up. We want to make a 'beurre noisette', or brown butter. This is when the whey solids cook and brown, giving the butter a nutty taste. When it goes brown, squeeze in the lemon juice and add the parsley. Season. Spoon quickly on the toast and devour.

HENRY'S TIPS

A glass of prosecco doesn't go amiss here. Try breadcrumbing and frying herring roes like fish fingers – absolutely delicious.

PÂTÉ DE CAMPAGNE

• 1.2KG •

A good coarse pâté is surprisingly easy to make, and a cut above what you can typically buy, not least because you know what went in. Get your friendly butcher to mince the ingredients for you. The pâté will taste better after a couple of days in the fridge.

1 shallot, diced	500g minced pork, quite fatty	pinch of ground coriander
1 garlic clove	250g minced bacon off-cuts	salt and pepper
1 sprig of thyme	1 egg	100g caul fat
100ml white wine	20g chopped parsley	**TO SERVE:**
20ml brandy	pinch of cayenne	2 slices of toasted sourdough and plenty of cornichons
500g minced pig's liver	pinch of mace	

1 Place the chopped shallot, garlic and thyme in a pan with the white wine. Heat up and reduce the wine to a syrup. Pour in the brandy and boil quickly. You want a small amount of cooked boozy onions with little liquid. Remove from the pan and cool. Discard the thyme.

2 Mix the minced liver, pork and bacon with the egg, parsley, spices and seasoning. Stir in the cooked shallot. You should have a sticky wet mixture.

3 Take a terrine mould or large loaf tin and line it carefully with the caul fat: you want plenty overhanging the sides. This gives the pâté a blanket so it doesn't dry out, and it looks nice as well. Spoon the mixture inside and wrap the caul fat over the top. Place the lid on top or wrap tightly in tin foil.

4 Heat the oven to 130°C and place the terrine mould in a baking tray surrounded with hot water. This helps the pâté to cook more evenly. It will take about 1–1½ hours to cook. If you have a temperature probe, take the pâté to an internal temperature of 68°C.

5 Remove from the oven and the water, and drain off a little of the excess fat from the tin. Find a similar-sized tin, or cut a piece of cardboard to the correct size and wrap it in foil, place on top and weigh it down with something heavy. The heavier the better (within reason) as you want a dense texture that doesn't crumble when cut. Put in a fridge to firm up overnight. To remove the pâté, fill an oven tray with boiling water and put the terrine mould in to loosen the fat, then, using a pallet knife, carefully release the pâté. Wrap in cling film and place in the fridge to chill again.

CASSOULET BEANS ON TOAST

FEEDS 1

When making a cassoulet (see page 222), it is worthwhile doing a few extra beans as they are wonderful the next day warmed up on toast. All those meaty juices and garlic flavours, with the odd bit of bacon, and confit duck if you're lucky, are great too. A fried egg wouldn't be a bad idea either.

2 slices of sourdough	200g cassoulet beans	1 egg, optional

1 Toast the sourdough. Heat the beans up in a pan, adding a little water to loosen them slightly and stop them catching on the base. When hot, pour over the toast.

2 Serve with a fried egg if you feel naughty.

BEEF STEW

• FEEDS 6 •

The perfect way to eat sourdough is with a rich braise, using the bread
as a spoon to mop up all the juices. Edible cutlery is the best.

1 sourdough loaf	2 garlic cloves, chopped	1 bay leaf
2kg ox cheeks, cubed	1 carrot, chopped	1 tsp Worcestershire sauce
20g flour	200ml red wine	1 tsp sherry vinegar
salt and pepper	1 litre chicken stock	1 tsp sugar
20ml oil	1 pig's trotter	
2 onions, chopped	1 sprig of thyme	

1 Dust the cubed ox cheeks in seasoned flour. Heat a frying pan, add the oil and brown the cheeks till dark. Remove the cheeks, and in the same pan fry the onions. When soft, add the garlic and carrot.

2 Deglaze with the wine and reduce, then add the stock, trotter and herbs. Bring to the boil and take off the heat.

3 Heat the oven to 120°C. Place the cheeks and their liquid in an oven dish. Put the lid on and cook in the oven for 6 hours, or until the meat is tender and succulent. Take out of the oven and remove the meat carefully. The trotter has done its work, adding a gelatinous, unctuous quality to the stew, and can be discarded. Simmer the sauce to reduce it until it is of a coating consistency (about two-thirds reduced). Taste and adjust the flavour with the Worcestershire sauce, sherry vinegar and sugar. Pour over the cheek and, using a hunk of sourdough as a spoon, sop up all those juices.

Never boil the meat – that makes it dry out and toughen. If it goes over 100°C, the moisture evaporates, but cooked gently the muscle simply breaks down, and the result is tender and juicy. If you can't get a trotter, don't worry, it's just a bonus. If not ox cheek, then shin, diced chuck or short ribs would all be perfect.

HENRY'S TIPS

TRENCHER WITH RIB OF BEEF

FEEDS 6 TO 9

A trencher is a medieval custom of using old bread as a plate to serve a dish upon. The bread was used to mop up juices, and often given to paupers as alms. To roast a truly magnificent rib of beef, then rest it on the base of a large sourdough loaf and serve it at the centre of a table, is a fine thing. Edible crockery is better still.

the base of a Hobbs House Shepherds Loaf, or other large sourdough, half an inch thick	3-bone rib of beef, as aged as possible: get the butcher to French trim it and remove the chine bone	salt and pepper plenty of horseradish

1 Heat the oven to 220°C. Season the outside of the rib and place in the hot oven for 20 minutes to brown all over. When it's looking good, turn the heat down to 180°C and continue to roast for 2–3 hours. I like my rib medium rare, rather than rare, as there is a lot of fat and it's nice if some renders down. The best way to check if the beef is done is to use a thermometer probe: take the beef to 55–60°C in the centre. Remove and rest for at least 40 minutes. It will continue to cook a little out of the oven.

2 Place the beef on the trencher and rest in a warm place. All the juices will soak into the bread-plate.

3 Remove the beef and carve on a chopping board. Lay the sliced beef back on the trencher and serve to a ravenous hoard, with liberal amounts of horseradish.

HENRY'S TIPS

A big topside or rolled sirloin will also work. Slice the beef thinly so it will be more tender.

TRENCHER WITH HANGER STEAK AND WARM MUSHROOM AND WATERCRESS SALAD

FEEDS 4

My dear friend and talented chef, Chris Redmond, showed me this lovely dish. It's so simple and quick. I've even cooked it leaning outside a tent in the pouring rain, it's that easy. It uses hanger steak, a delightful cut that hangs on the inside of the beef carcass, hence the name. It is classified as offal and is similar to skirting steak. The flesh is dark and loose-textured and has a deep beefy flavour. I have to say that it is my steak of choice, and it costs a fraction compared to other steaks.

4 thick slices of sourdough	30g butter	small bunch of parsley, chopped
1 large hanger or onglet steak, totally trimmed of sinew	3 garlic cloves, crushed	large bunch of watercress, trimmed
	12 chestnut mushrooms, cut into quarters	
salt and pepper		2 shallots, thinly sliced
20g oil	30g sherry vinegar	Dijon mustard, to serve

1 Season the hanger steak liberally. Heat the oven to 120°C. Heat a large frying pan till it is smoking hot. Add the oil and quickly brown the hanger steak really well. Meanwhile, toast the sourdough. Place the toast on an oven tray in a close line, like soldiers side by side. Remove the hanger from the pan and lay on top of the sourdough. Place in the oven for 30 minutes to rest and finish cooking through very gently. Hanger is best served pink and well rested. Cooked any longer and it would get dry and tough due to its lack of fat.

2 Don't wash the frying pan, but save it for the mushrooms. When the steak has been resting for 25 minutes, reheat the pan and add the butter. When melted, gently fry the garlic. Then add the mushrooms and turn the heat up. Season and cook till brown and soft. Deglaze with the vinegar and add the chopped parsley. Toss around and pour into a salad bowl. Mix in the watercress and sliced shallot. Give it a good toss: you want the heat of the mushroom to slightly wilt the watercress. Season to taste.

3 Remove the hanger from the trenchers and slice thinly against the grain. Put a juice-soaked trencher on each plate and lay the sliced hanger on top. Serve with the warm salad and mustard.

SOURDOUGH PANCAKES

·——— · MAKES 8 MEDIUM-SIZED PANCAKES · ———·

Shrove Tuesday, Mardi Gras, Fettisdagen, Fat Tuesday, whatever you call it, the last day before Ash Wednesday (the first day of Lent) is *Pancake Day*! And all over the world, people celebrate by using up fat and eggs in the best way they can before forty days of edifying (but optional) abstinence.

England used to mark the occasion with an official half-day, working until 11 a.m., and then after church the rest of the day was taken off to scoff pancakes. In Scotland, a festy cock, a pancake-shaped patty, is baked in the hot ashes of a mill kiln to mark Shrovetide. In Hawaii the day is known as Malasada Day, and they eat the sweet fried doughnuts that give the day its name. Closer to home for us, in Olney, Buckinghamshire, the residents have a pancake race. This is run by the women of the town in memory of a cook in 1445 who, on hearing the Shriving Bell, ran out of the house in her headscarf and apron and arrived at church still clutching the frying pan she had been using to make pancakes. The prize for the fastest lady in the pancake race? A kiss from the verger. This day has some flippin' hot heritage.

In the Herbert house, this special tiny Tuesday seems to spring up on us, and like the first snowdrop, heralds a new season. We make a triple batch, pile them high on a big plate and serve them, still steaming, to play the part of an edible scroll to delicious savoury and sweet fillings. Sourdough gives the pancakes a depth of flavour that is perfect with both dinner and pudding courses. Some sourdough regimes sourly suggest you pour surplus dough down the sink. Not any more: let a surfeit of sourdough spark a pancake party. Great any time of year, guaranteed.

1 Break three whole eggs into a large bowl and whisk. Add 170ml whole milk and 120ml sourdough, two 2-finger pinches of salt, 100g plain white flour and whisk all together. Then, melt a big knob of butter in a large frying pan and whisk into the pancake batter.

2 Now, fry the pancakes in the large frying pan, tossing occasionally until they are golden on both sides. Lubricate your frying pan between pancakes with a little oil on kitchen paper. Serve while still warm.

SOURDOUGH AND SODA BREAD

SOURDOUGH PANCAKES WITH POACHED FRUIT AND CRÈME FRAICHE

• FEEDS 4 •

I can't resist the temptation of warm poached fruit with crème fraîche on a sourdough pancake. Such a delightful combination, and worthy of any brunch menu.

4 sourdough pancakes, freshly cooked	1 orange, zested and juiced	50g blueberries
	1 vanilla pod, halved lengthways	**TO SERVE:**
FOR THE POACHING LIQUOR:	**FOR THE FRUIT:**	100g crème fraîche
150g sugar	100g strawberries, hulled	30g toasted flaked almonds
200ml water	100g redcurrants, destalked	

1 Put all the poaching ingredients into a pan and bring to a gentle simmer. Taste: it should be sweet with a slight tang from the orange.

2 Add the fruit and heat gently for 3 minutes, then remove from the heat and allow the fruit to wallow in the liquor for as long as possible. This will keep for a week in the fridge.

3 To serve, gently warm the fruit in a little liquor, spoon generously over the pancakes and dollop the crème fraîche on. Sprinkle a few toasted almonds over for a nice crunchy top.

Sourdough pancakes are also great with maple syrup and bacon.

HENRY'S TIPS

SPICY MERGUEZ SAUSAGE WITH TOMATO, SPINACH AND SOURDOUGH PANCAKES

• FEEDS 4 •

There is a great little Algerian restaurant in Brixton that serves these wonderful pancakes for breakfast. I used to go there once a week when I lived in London to indulge in the spicy sausage and a black rosewater coffee. Most decent butchers will make merguez, a beef and mutton sausage spiced with paprika.

4 sourdough pancakes, freshly cooked	2 garlic cloves, sliced	100g baby spinach
	6 ripe tomatoes, coarsely chopped	salt and pepper
20ml olive oil		1 tsp chopped parsley
8 thin merguez sausages	1 tsp smoked paprika	4 poached eggs (optional)
1 onion, thinly sliced	1 tsp red wine vinegar	

1 Heat a frying pan with half the olive oil and gently brown the merguez sausages. They will release a lovely red oil as you do so. When they have browned nicely, remove and set aside. Add the remaining oil and quickly fry the onion and garlic. After about 5 minutes, add the chopped tomatoes and give it a mix. As the tomato juices reduce down into the onions, reintroduce the merguez and cover with a lid.

2 After 15 minutes, check on proceedings, sprinkle in the paprika and red wine vinegar, let it bubble, then add the spinach. As the spinach cooks down it will release lots of water. Simmer gently till the mixture is thick and sauce-like, taste for seasoning and sprinkle in the parsley. Spoon onto the warm sourdough pancakes. I'm quite partial to a poached egg at this stage, but I leave that to your discretion.

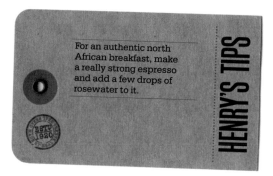

For an authentic north African breakfast, make a really strong espresso and add a few drops of rosewater to it.

HENRY'S TIPS

ESTD 1920

SODA BREAD

• MAKES 1 LOAF •

Soda bread – bread raised by bicarbonate of soda, rather than yeast – comes from Ireland, where these instant loaves were baked in heavy pots over peat fires with a cross cut in the top. This was supposed to keep the devil out, but it also means you can divide them into four handy rolls. Traditionally, buttermilk (a byproduct of butter making) is used to make soda bread. It is more acidic than normal milk, and that's good because it reacts really well with the bicarbonate, which is alkaline, and you get a better rise in the bread. (If you want to go the whole hog, you can make your own butter and buttermilk: see page 166.) I use baking powder, which is a mixture of bicarbonate of soda and cream of tartar, and for flour my recipe here calls for wholemeal spelt. This is easier to digest than conventional wheat flour, an important consideration with such a speedy bread. Also it has a luscious nutty flavour that works an absolute treat.

300g wholemeal spelt flour	flour for dusting	Scraper
a big pinch of sea salt	**KIT**	Oven gloves
2 tsp baking powder	Oven and baking stone: 230°C	
230ml buttermilk (home-made if desired; see page 166)	Set of scales, preferably digital	
	Large mixing bowl	

1 Once you have the oven and baking stone heated to 230°C, and all your ingredients and kit to hand, weigh the dry ingredients into the bowl and blend together.

2 Add the buttermilk and, using the scraper, mix the ingredients together for about 2 minutes, checking there are no dry bits at the bottom. The moment all the ingredients have mixed together and you have a sticky dough, flour the work surface and tip the dough onto it. Then, cupping the dough between your floury hands, shape it into a round and place directly onto your baking stone.

3 Using the scraper, cut a cross deeply into the dough and bake for 15–20 minutes, until your soda bread has a great golden crust and sounds hollow when tapped on the bottom.

Have your oven hot and work fast to get your loaf baking before the bicarbonate of soda in the baking powder runs out of gas. This will help ensure your soda bread is light and delicious. Go with the very wet dough in the recipe. The bran in the wholemeal will carry on absorbing the buttermilk after you've put it in the oven.

TOM'S TIPS

Organic Wholemeal

SHEPHERD'S LOAF

HOBBS HOUSE   THE PERFECT LOAF

pelt

Organic White

Organic Oatmeal

Tabatiere

Organic Light Rye sourdough

Organic Soda bread

Organic Soda Seeds

Organic Wild White

MAKING YOUR OWN BUTTER AND BUTTERMILK

FOR 230ML BUTTERMILK

To make 230ml buttermilk, beat 700ml double cream fast until the sound changes and it properly separates into curds of butter and watery buttermilk. (Those of you who've overwhipped cream may not have known you were just moments away from making home-made butter.) You'll know exactly when you've reached the right stage. Sieve the curds out over a big bowl, squash them down a bit to get all the milk out, then plop the curds into very cold water. With a firm hand, squish the curds together underwater to make a rough ball of butter. Place on a piece of greaseproof paper and roll it up. You now have a luscious pack of your own hand-made butter to savour, melted over a slice of warm soda bread. You also have, in the big bowl, the acidic buttermilk, perfect for making soda bread.

FLAVOURINGS

Unsalted butter keeps for only a few days. For salted butter (which lasts longer), weigh the butter before shaping, and add 2 per cent of the weight in sea salt flakes by just rubbing it through. You could also add chopped fresh herbs, such as tarragon or parsley, or chopped chillies or garlic.

BUTTERMILK ALTERNATIVES

If you don't have buttermilk or the cream to make it with, you can sour ordinary milk with the juice of half a lemon – just squeeze it into the milk and stir it in. Or you can sour milk at room temperature for 3 days prior to baking. This will cause the milk to turn yogurty and acidic. It can smell proper whiffy, but in my opinion makes the best and creamiest (if you use whole milk) soda bread in the world.

OATY BLACK TREACLE SODA BREAD

This bread has a beguiling sweetness. Follow the soda bread recipe on page 162, but replace 50g of the wholemeal spelt flour with 50g oats, and replace 80ml of the buttermilk with 50g black treacle loosened in 2 tablespoons hot water (weight: 80g). Weigh them into the mix at the same time as the other ingredients, and roll the dough in oats instead of flour for a stunning oaty flaky finish to a slightly sweet loaf. It takes a little longer to bake: about 25 minutes altogether.

HOBBS HOUSE SODA SEEDS

Make the soda bread recipe as on page 162, adding 50g of mixed seeds: sesame, poppy, sunflower, pumpkin and linseed work well. Then roll the loaf in seeds and bake in a small bread tin. This loaf is popular in the bakery, and is very good when thinly sliced and toasted to eat with excellent cheese and pâté.

FETA AND THYME SODA

Add 50g crumbled feta cheese and a small handful of thyme leaves pulled off their stalks to the soda bread recipe along with the dry ingredients, for a tasty loaf that needs no accompaniment.

WHITE HONEY SODA

Diggin' the yeast-free soda but fancy a lighter loaf? Try replacing the wholemeal spelt with white flour (or refined spelt flour: it's lighter, with some of the bran removed), drop the liquid content back to 180ml and add 30ml of honey.

SMOKED MACKEREL PÂTÉ

• MAKES 250G •

This pâté is so quick, you can knock it up while your soda bread is baking and slather it on while it's still warm.

200g smoked mackerel fillets	juice of ½ lemon	salt and pepper
50g crème fraîche	5g chopped parsley	

1 Carefully peel the skin from the mackerel fillets. Using your nails, pick out the bones running down the centre of each fillet. Flake into chunks. Depending on whether you like smooth or coarse, make them small or large. I like a little texture and not a mash so I leave mine quite large.

2 Add the remaining ingredients and gently fold through. Check for seasoning. A little lemon goes a long way. Serve with warm soda bread and some pickled beetroot.

HENRY'S TIPS

Serve with a beetroot and dressed watercress salad. Smoked trout works equally well in this recipe. A spoonful of horseradish sauce can give the pâté a subtle kick: smoked fish and horseradish were meant for one another.

POTTED SHRIMP

MAKES 400G

The humble brown shrimp is often overlooked for bigger, meatier cousins, but these little things have power in numbers. They are sweet and delicate but with enough flavour to keep you coming back for more. They go great with soda bread.

250g butter	juice of ½ lemon	
1 blade of mace	pinch of cayenne	
2 peelings of lemon rind	salt and pepper	
250g brown shrimps, cooked and peeled	cucumber pickles (see page 190), to serve	

1 Gently melt the butter with the mace and lemon rind until it separates. Scum will float to the top. Remove this with a spoon. The salty wheys will sink. The pure fat in the middle is clarified butter. This is what we want.

2 When the butter has been infusing for 40 minutes or so, ladle off the clarified butter into a bowl, keeping a few ladles back for later use. Add the brown shrimps while the butter is still warm. Mix together, add the lemon juice and cayenne and season with salt and pepper. Spoon the mixture into four small pots (100–120ml). Place in the fridge to firm up. When firm, spoon on a top layer of the butter you set aside to seal all the shrimps in.

3 These will last for a couple of weeks in the fridge. To serve, take them out of the fridge 20 minutes before you need them to take the chill off, and spread on top of freshly baked soda bread or steaming soda toast. Cucumber pickles don't go amiss here either.

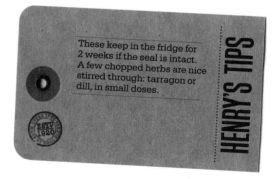

These keep in the fridge for 2 weeks if the seal is intact. A few chopped herbs are nice stirred through: tarragon or dill, in small doses.

HENRY'S TIPS

ENRICHED DOUGHS

THE JEWELS IN OUR BAKERY CROWN

If sourdough be the king, then surely brioche is the queen of breads. The humble dough takes on a regal stature with every knob of butter and rich yolk added until it can hold no more. The ultimate in enriched dough, and perhaps the most glamorous of breads. 'Qu'ils mangent de la brioche,' said Marie Antoinette, allegedly.

As spring becomes summer, and the fire of desire grows in us to cook and eat outside, so too does the need for some seriously decent burger baps and hotdog rolls. After too many bad bap experiences, I took myself into the Hobbs bakehouse and imaginarium, from which I emerged some time later in a puff of flour with… the ultimate burger bap.

Lardy cake is big in Gloucestershire. We've done it for ever in the bakery, and people will travel for it. Seriously, this is a proper cake, made with relatively cheap ingredients and developed in an era when ploughmen and labourers burnt a lot of calories. It's a beautiful blend of pure lard and sugar with juicy raisins, folded into a basic bread dough and baked in such a way that it caramelises on the bottom to a shiny soft toffee finish. Y-U-M-M! WARNING: eat responsibly…

BRIOCHE

MAKES 1 LARGE OR 2 SMALL LOAVES

A brioche is a brilliant thing of beauty, each slice divine.

500g strong white flour	300g butter (half an hour out of the fridge)	Small loaf tins, or large and small fluted tins if you have them
10g sea salt		
20g caster sugar	**KIT**	Scraper
75g cold water	Set of scales, preferably digital	Oven and baking stone: 210°C at baking time
5g dried yeast (or 10g fresh yeast if you can get it)	Large mixing bowl or mixer with dough hook	
4 medium eggs	Cling film or a disposable shower cap	
4 medium yolks, plus 1 extra, beaten, to glaze		

1 Set the butter to one side and weigh all the ingredients into a mixing bowl. Mix a firm dough, 10 minutes in a mixer with the hook, or 15 minutes hard at it by hand.

2 With the dough on the worktop, dice the butter into small cubes, then knead the butter cubes in one by one. This is a time-consuming labour of love for a demanding but mightily regally rewarding loaf. Once all the butter is in, the dough will be soft as a queen's pillow, but curiously not sticky.

3 Return the dough to the mixing bowl and cover. Leave it overnight in the fridge to rest and rise.

4 Next day, using the scraper, get the buttery dough out of the bowl.

FOR A BRIOCHE WITH TOP KNOT

1 Weigh a kilo of dough. Twist off a top knot bit (about 2/5ths, being fussy). Butter the inside of a large, 900g round fluted tin (melt a little butter and pastry-brush it on or use kitchen paper). Mould both pieces of dough into tight round balls. Place the largest one in the bottom of the tin, with the seam/knot on the bottom, then place the top knot on top. Flour, then, if you like, push your two biggest fingers deep into the brioche from above. This'll keep the top bun from slipping off, and yield you a brioche that is neat and pert, with curves in all the right places. Brush the top with a beaten egg yolk (the queen of glossy glazes).

2 Once the brioche is in the tin, cover it, taking care to see that the cover doesn't come into contact with the delicate dough. (This is where the shower cap comes in handy.) Leave the covered tin in a warm place to rise. Once it has doubled in size (or the outside edge of the dough is only a touch under the rim of the tin), bake in a 210°C oven on a heated baking stone.

3 After 5 minutes, turn the oven temperature down to 160°C and bake until golden: about 45 minutes.

FOR A SMALL LOAF TIN

Weigh a 500g piece and divide it into 3. With only the lightest sprinkling of flour, shape them into round rolls and place them in a small buttered loaf tin. If there is a slightly larger lump, this can go in the middle. Glaze as on page 177 and continue with the main recipe instructions. In step 3, bake for 35 minutes.

FOR BRIOCHE ROLLS

If you have some little fluted tins, butter them, and divide the dough into 50g pieces. Place the dough in the buttered tins. Glaze as on page 177 and continue with the main recipe instructions. In step 3, bake for 15 minutes.

If your brioche should start to catch and burn before it's baked, cover it with foil. And take note: no steam! Steam is great for a crust, but Marie Antoinette says no to crust on this one.

TOM'S TIPS

DUCK LIVER PARFAIT

· MAKES ABOUT 1KG ·

BUT IT KEEPS WELL FOR A WEEK, OR SERVE IT TO A CROWD

Rich duck livers laden with butter and finished with brandy, a parfait to make the hardest of guests swoon in sheer delight. Don't skimp on the booze, it makes all the difference to that first bite.

2 shallots, finely diced	500g butter	pinch of cayenne pepper
1 sprig of thyme	500g fresh duck livers	pinch of saltpetre (ask your butcher)
100ml port	1 egg yolk	
30ml brandy	20g salt	pinch of white pepper

1 Put the shallots and thyme in a small pan. Pour in the port, bring to the boil, then gently simmer for 5 minutes, until the shallots are cooked and have taken on a lovely port colour. There should be little liquid left. Add the brandy and flambé the alcohol off, being careful of your eyebrows. Take off the heat and allow to cool.

2 In a separate pan, gently melt the butter, then skim off any foam that rises to the top.

3 Place the duck livers in a food processor and add the remaining ingredients. Give it a good blitz to make a purple mush. Add the boozy shallots and keep blitzing. Now, whilst the motor is still running slowly, pour in the warm melted butter. It is important that the butter is warm, otherwise it may split. When all the butter is added and the mixture is smooth and silky, stop the processor and push the mixture through a fine sieve into a terrine mould or clean loaf tin.

4 Heat the oven to 120°C. Place the terrine mould in an oven tray with a few centimetres of water surrounding it. This helps to cook the parfait evenly. Place a lid on the terrine mould or cover with foil and place in the oven. The parfait will take about 45 minutes, but a probe thermometer is very useful as you want the parfait to reach 68°C and no further. As soon as it has reached 68°C, remove from the oven and take it out of the water.

5 Melt a little butter and pour on top of the parfait to seal it. Place in the fridge overnight before eating. It keeps for a week, and is best on about day three. Serve with warm brioche.

HENRY'S TIPS

The saltpetre keeps the parfait pink but is not essential. It also makes the skin itch, so if you do have it, wear gloves. This parfait tastes better after 3 days.

ENRICHED DOUGHS

179

BREAD AND BUTTER PUDDING

· FEEDS 4 ·

A classic pudding, using the brioche to add a new richness
without becoming too sweet.

5 slices of brioche	3 yolks	1 vanilla pod, split, and seeds scraped out with the point of a knife
50g soft butter	50g sugar	
20g raisins	300ml cream	
3 eggs	300ml milk	

1 Butter the brioche on both sides. Scatter the raisins into an oven dish. Place the slices of brioche on top. Mix the eggs, yolks, sugar, cream, milk and vanilla seeds, and pour over the brioche. Dunk the slices a few times to drown them.

2 Let the pudding sit for 20 minutes before baking, so the custard soaks into the bread. Heat the oven to 120°C. Place in the oven for 30 minutes or until the custard has set. Serve while still warm.

Vanilla extract is a suitable substitute for vanilla seeds from a pod, but not quite the same. Keep vanilla pods in the fridge; they last longer. Place used pods in the sugar jar to make vanilla sugar. Some orange zest and a shot of brandy in the custard can lift spirits on a cold day.

HENRY'S TIPS

ULTIMATE BURGER BAP

• MAKES 10 •

The choice of the meat on offer at farmers' markets and summer festivals has grown enormously, in line with our desire for good husbandry, impeccable provenance and fine quality. But why are baps so pappy? I'd often rather eat my perfectly seasoned, hot meat patty in the wrapping it came in. So one day I closed my eyes and visualized, there on my culinary horizon, a beautiful golden bun. Pert and well risen, with a touch of sweetness and a hint of sourdough. Glazed as delicately as a nightingale's egg, its golden shell adorned with a sprinkle of sesame seeds. And so the ultimate burger bap was born at the Hobbs House bakery, and officially launched in 2011 at Bristol's international barbecuing festival, Grillstock. It has risen to become one of our most popular products ever. Here's how to make them at home. Moulded into a different shape, this is also the ultimate hotdog finger bun.

500g strong white flour	beaten egg, to glaze	
200ml tepid milk	sesame seeds, to finish	
100ml tepid water	**KIT**	
25g caster sugar	Set of scales	
25g lard	Mixing bowl or mixer with hook	
25g sourdough (optional)	Cling film or a disposable shower cap	
10g salt	Scraper	
5g dried yeast (or 10g fresh yeast if you can get it)	Oven and baking stone: 230°C at baking time	

1 Weigh all the ingredients into a bowl and mix thoroughly. Knead for 10 minutes in the mixer with a hook, or 15 minutes by hand. Leave to rise in a covered bowl for an hour in a warm place.

2 Divide the dough into 10 pieces and roll out 10cm baps on a floured surface. (Or make 10 hotdog finger buns.) Place on a baking tray lined with baking parchment. Brush beaten egg over each bap. Leave in a warm place for an hour to rise.

3 Sprinkle sesame seeds on each bap and leave for a further half hour to rise. Bake your baps until they are perfectly golden: about 10–15 minutes.

To make hotdog finger rolls, make the dough round, as with the baps, then roll them back and forth into a sausage shape to the length you desire. For an exquisite glaze crust, after 30 minutes' rising, brush the rolls/baps with a second coating of beaten egg.

TOM'S TIPS

FRANKFURTERS

I felt it was about time to show all how an authentic hotdog can be as good, if not better, than its round beefy cousin. The frankfurter is the key element. A shop-bought one will just not do. Making your own is not as hard as it seems and will reward you hugely later on. It also means building a smoker, which is über cool and has many culinary delights in store.

750g pork shoulder, boned and de-rinded	5g white pepper and ground coriander	250g cold water
500g hard back fat	pinch of saltpetre	natural sausage skins, soaked in cold water
15g salt	3g ground mace	

1 Mince the pork shoulder and back fat through a fine mincer twice to get a smooth result. Either do this yourself or get your butcher to do it for you. Mix in the remaining dry ingredients. Be careful with the saltpetre; it makes the skin itch.

2 Place the mixture in a Kitchen Aid on the paddle attachment and turn it on a low setting. Pour the cold water in slowly; you want to beat the water into the mixture to form a smooth mousse that is light and fluffy.

3 Using a sausage stuffer (or a funnel, which is way harder and more frustrating), fill the machine and slide the soaked sausage skins fully over the nozzle. Turn the handle of the machine slowly till the sausage meat is protruding out of the end, pull a section of skin over the protrusion and tie a knot. Now slowly turn the handle and feed the sausages into the skins. An even pace is needed so you don't overfill and split the skins, or end up with saggy wieners.

4 When you have one long continuous sausage, you can create hotdogs of the desired size by gently pinching along the length to form gaps and twisting into shape. Place in the fridge to firm up overnight.

5 Now for the smoking. Load your home-made smoker (see opposite) with oak or other hardwood chips. Turn the heat on and put the chamber on top. Hang the frankfurters, evenly spaced, and allow to smoke for about 3–6 hours. When done, the sausages will have gained a slight suntan bronzing. There will also be beads of moisture on the surface.

6 Remove from the smoker and put in the fridge for at least 2 days to mellow the harsh smoke flavour. The sausages will last for a week in a fridge.

HOW TO MAKE A SMOKER

What could be better than a slightly bodged contraption that allows you to fill either your kitchen or your garage with wafting bellows of oak smoke? Hot smoking is what chefs do with silly trays of rice and sugar and tea bags to make a piece of chicken or fish taste slightly rubbery and harsh; cold smoking, however, is cool. It doesn't cook the ingredients but slowly imparts a beautiful smoky flavour and a wonderful colour. I have smoked all sorts of things since I started on my hazy quest, from sausages to butter to cream to my arm. Things that are salty or fatty seem to attract the smoke more. The great thing about smoked products is that they last longer, so a smoked sausage will last twice as long as a normal one.

1 Making your own is really easy and far from costly. First you need a small portable electric hob or gas stove: the worse it is, the better, as it doesn't need to get that hot. Then you need a 20-litre metal oil drum – ask your local chippie for an old one of theirs. Using a tin opener, cut the top off and give it a quick clean. If there are any jagged edges, use a metal file to smooth them down. (Nothing worse than a sharp tin cut.) Then you need a large plastic black bin with a lid. The cheap ones from hardware stores are fine. They sit perfectly on the top of the oil drum. Using a drill, punch a few holes in the base. This allows the smoke to trickle from the drum into the bin. Finally, you need a long sturdy length of wooden dowel. Turn the bin on its side and near the top, just below the rim, drill two holes on opposite sides. Cut the dowel slightly longer than the bin width then push it through one hole and out the other. This makes a rail to hang stuff on.

2 All you need now are the chips. You can buy smoking chips online but they tend to be expensive. A saw mill or timber merchant can be a good source of material, if you have one locally. However, it's important you use only hardwoods. The aroma of pine, for example, is harsh and imparts a bitter flavour. My preferences are for oak, hickory, cherry and ash. Never use treated wood.

3 To use, place the drum on the hob and turn it on low. Sprinkle a handful of chips in the bottom. A little goes a long way. Place the bin on top. Hang your sausages from the dowel and put on the lid. Sausages take about 3 hours of constant smoke and a ham can take 2 days. Keep an eye on it every hour or so to see how the chips are doing. Add more if it's running thin or turn the heat up to give it a blast. But basically have fun and smoke away. It opens up a world of possibilities.

HOTDOGS

To cook the hotdogs, heat a pan of water to a gentle simmer. Put the sausages into the water and poach for 15 minutes until cooked through. Now to assemble the dog.

4 ultimate finger buns (see the ultimate burger bap, page 182)	1 onion, sliced	1 bottle French's American mustard
4 hotdog frankfurters (page 184)	1 tsp Worcestershire sauce	
1 tbsp oil	salt and pepper	
	cucumber pickles (page 190)	

1 Heat the oil in a frying pan and quickly fry the sliced onion. When they are colouring nicely, add the Worcestershire sauce. Season and remove from the heat. Wipe the pan out, then gently brown the hotdogs in it. I like mine to be crispy on the outside. They will take about 10 minutes to heat through.

2 Take the buns and cut open. Fill with onions and pickles. Lay the hotdog on top and drizzle the French's mustard artfully on top.

HENRY'S TIPS

Always open a hotdog roll by cutting along the top, never along the side.

It is not essential to fry the dog, but the skin on poached frankfurters can be quite tough, and frying breaks the skin down. I also just happen to like a crispy sausage.

SLIDER BURGERS

• FEEDS 4 •

How often do you go into a self-proclaimed upmarket gastro pub and see something like: *The King's Arms 8oz Angus burger on toasted ciabatta with relish and chips*? It all sounds so good, then out comes a wooden board with the largest amount of cheap bread in the middle, a stick poking out of the top and no sign of the burger. Is it so hard to make a burger with the meat patty and the bun the same size? And not only that, but does it really need to be so over-filled and high that a stick is needed to hold the darn thing together and it's impossible to get into your mouth without splitting your lips?

Here I have the answer. On the advice of my friend Marcus of aintnopicnicburgers, I give you: the Slider. The juiciest, meatiest, 'oh my goodness I could never eat any other burger' burger. This uses chuck steak – I make it from the best rare breed British beef, hung properly for a month – paired with Tom's ultimate burger bun, a slice of burger cheese and a few home-made pickles. It will be a revelation to all burger lovers out there.

4 ultimate burger baps	salt and pepper	1 big ripe tomato, sliced
400g chuck steak, minced	1 onion, very thinly sliced	butterhead lettuce
2 tbsp oil	4 slices burger cheese	cucumber pickles (see overleaf)

1 Divide the mince into 4 equal balls and lightly roll. The idea behind a slider is that you don't season and mix the burger, which will cause the meat to dry out and cure. Instead you season it last minute like a steak, so it retains maximum juiciness.

2 Heat a frying pan and when smoking hot add the oil and the round balls of mince. Season and allow to brown for 1 minute, then push a small pinch of onions into the middle of each ball and 'slam' the burger flat with a pallet knife. Flip the burger over so the onions can brown off and melt into the meat. Cook for a further 2 minutes, or longer if you don't like pink. Serve in baps with butterhead lettuce, ripe tomato and pickled cucumber. Or do as I do: place a piece of cheese and the split bun on top of the burger still in the pan, so the cheese melts to the bun. Lift the burger and add the bottom of the bun. Enjoy the juiciest, most chin-drippingly delicious burger ever.

I'm partial to cheap cheese on a burger, but use a better one if you must. Any tomato you use, however, needs to be ripe and tasty. Particularly delicious with a slider burger, I find, are home-made cucumber pickles (see overleaf).

HENRY'S TIPS

CUCUMBER PICKLES

These are based on an old recipe I once came across, where they were called 'bread and butter pickles'.

1 cucumber, thinly sliced	100g caster sugar	small bunch of dill
10g sea salt	25ml water	
100ml white wine vinegar	1 tsp mustard seeds	

1 In a bowl, sprinkle the salt over the cucumber and mix. Leave for 30 minutes to draw the water out.

2 Meanwhile, heat the vinegar, sugar, water and mustard seeds. Remove from the heat and chill. Add the dill when cold.

3 Wash the cucumber of any salt for a few minutes under a cold tap. Then add to the pickle. Leave at least 12 hours, but a couple of days is best. Will keep for a couple of weeks in the fridge.

These cucumber pickles are great in the burger (see page 188) or on the side with potted shrimp (see page 170). Using the same method, try carrots peeled into ribbons, sliced mushrooms such as ceps, or beetroot that's been boiled, peeled and chopped. A row of jars of pickles looks amazing on a shelf.

HENRY'S TIPS

CHALLAH

A rich and irresistible bread with a fine story, and a super delicious centrepiece for any well-laid table. The bread plays a central part in the ceremony of the Sabbath meal, which begins with two loaves, over which blessings are said. To make challah, you should allow three hours.

600g strong white flour	2 eggs, keeping 1 yolk for glaze	Scraper
10g sea salt	handful of poppy seeds	High-sided roasting tin
7g dried yeast (or 15g fresh yeast if you can get it)	**KIT**	Oven and baking stone: 210°C at baking time
	Set of scales, preferably digital	
270ml warm water	Large mixing bowl or mixer with dough hook	Pastry brush and pot for egg yolk
30g caster sugar		
50g soft butter	Cling film	

1 Weigh the ingredients into the mixing bowl and mix together for 10 minutes with a dough hook, or turn out and knead for 15 minutes by hand, until you have a creamy, stretchy, smooth and elastic dough. Put it back in the bowl, cover with cling film and leave to double in size in a warm place, or for an hour, whichever comes first.

2 Then use the scraper to ease the dough out of the bowl. With the scraper, divide the dough into three roughly equal pieces. Roll out each dough piece into a tapered sausage shape, then plait them together.

3 Place the loaf in the roasting tin. Glaze the plait with the egg yolk and top the loaf with poppy seeds. Cover the tin with cling film and put the loaf in a warm place for its final rise.

4 While the loaf doubles in size (about half an hour), heat the oven and baking stone to 210°C. Carefully take off the cling film and slide the plait in its roasting tin onto the baking stone. Bake for about half an hour, until the challah is beautiful and golden.

Plait your loaf from the middle for an excellent shape. Watch carefully that the sugar in the loaf, which will give the plait a wonderful golden lustre, doesn't burn. Warning: it can happen quite quickly.

ESTD 1920

TOM'S TIPS

LARDY CAKE

Whenever I used to take a couple of slices of lardy cake home for my granddad, who lived opposite us, he'd always say, 'Lovely, but not quite as good as Ro Richards's!' (of Bicester Bakery lardy cake fame). Years later I met up with Ro, now aged ninety-four, and he offered to spend the day with me, showing me the way of the lardy. Ro is a tough master, a quietly assured craftsman; he had all the tools of his trade in an old leather doctor's bag, and he baked wearing a tie. After an epic morning, not only had Ro seen his recipe passed on, but he declared the lardies we made the best he'd ever tasted. This had a lot to do with rendering our own lard from good local Gloucester Old Spot pigs.

FOR THE DOUGH:	4g salt	100g currants
275g strong white bread flour	175ml warm water	
1 tbsp lard	**FOR THE LARD AND SUGAR MIX:**	
5g dried yeast (or 10g fresh yeast if you can get it)	250g caster sugar	
	200g lard, slightly softened	

1 Line two small (15cm) cake tins or enamel pie dishes with greaseproof paper.

2 Mix the dough as for the basic white dough (page 50). Leave in a covered bowl to rest for an hour. Meanwhile, mix the sugar in the lard using a wooden spoon.

3 Divide the dough in half and mould each into a round shape. On a well-floured table, roll each one out with a pin into two 20cm discs. Divide the lard and sugar mix into two.

4 Now, using a small pallet knife, spread two-thirds of each lard and sugar mix onto each dough disc, keeping one-third for the next stage. Spread it evenly to the edges, then fold. This requires you to take an outside edge and pull it into the middle, so that the circle has a straight edge with a corner at each end. Now take the bottom corner, pull it into the middle and push the dough down with your palm. Working clockwise, keep turning the dough, picking up the bottom corner and pulling it into the centre, until you've worked your way all round.

5 Rest the dough for 10 minutes, then roll the disc out to 20cm again and spread the remaining sweet lard mix on top. Now sprinkle with some currants and fold as before. Roll out to fit your lined cake tin. Put a big knob of lard on the bottom of the tin, on the paper, and spread it around to cover the bottom. Then sprinkle a generous tablespoon of sugar over the lard and place the lardy on top, with the flat side on the bottom and the layered, knotted side on top. Cover and leave in a warm place to rise. After an hour, or as soon as the lardy has proved to form a seal around the inside edge so you can no longer see the inside bottom of the tin, bake in a hot oven, 210°C, on a baking stone, until you can just lift the cake from the tin using a small pallet knife, and the cake is golden all over: about 30 minutes. Leave to cool in the tin for 10 minutes so the caramelised lard toffee has set a bit, then tip out onto greaseproof paper. The lardy is served sunny side up.

RENDERING YOUR OWN LARD

1 Get some good quality pork flare fat from your butcher, cut into big chunks and put into a roasting tin in a low oven (140°C) for a couple of hours. Using a slotted spoon, remove the firm bits that float in the hot liquid fat and throw them away. Pour the hot liquid quality pig fat into a bowl and leave it to set. It will go cloudy as it cools. Now you have some premium lard.

If the lard and sugar mix is hard to spread, warm it ever so slightly. In the oven, if the cake starts to burn on top, before it's golden underneath, cover the top with some kitchen foil. To mitigate against this, have a good hot baking stone underneath.

TOM'S TIPS

BUNS

I love hot-cross-bun time of year. (Easter, obviously. Lots of work
for us in the bakery, but also chocolate eggs, bank holidays, and fine
spring walks with the reward of a pot of tea and warm hot cross
buns slathered with too much butter at the end.) A split, toasted
and buttered hot cross bun with a good cup of tea can transform
a good Friday into an excellent one. It's one thing to buy them
from a bakery (never get those 12-for-£1 packs from a pallet in the
supermarket entrance), but to bake them at home is a very special
thing to do. I'm not sure there is a finer aroma in the whole of
bakingdom than spicy hot cross bunnies just out of the oven.

See page 201 for an elaborate and super-celebratory version
of the classic hot cross bun, and see page 200 for other
buns to make with the dough.

HOT CROSS BUNS

• MAKES 16 •

Back when I was wooing my wife Anna, I'd bake her three of these with
'I ♥ U' piped on top.

FOR THE DOUGH:

680g strong white flour

10g sea salt

15g dried yeast (or 30g fresh yeast if you can get it)

100g golden caster sugar

80g soft butter

15g mixed spice

175ml tepid whole milk

175ml tepid water

1 egg

FOR THE FRUIT:

80g sultanas

80g currants

the zest of 1 lemon and 1 orange

FOR THE CROSSING:

100g strong white flour, a pinch of salt, a pinch of sugar, a knob of butter and 100ml water

FOR THE BUN WASH:

1 eggcup of boiling water

2 tsp sugar

1 pinch of mixed spice

1 Weigh all the dough ingredients into a big mixing bowl. With a firm hand, stir together with a staunch wooden spoon. Turn the loose dough onto a bench and knead for a full 15 minutes until your dough is smooth and vital. (Or do it all in a mixer for 10 minutes.)

2 Gently work in the fruit and zest. Nestle your well-worked dough back into the big mixing bowl, cover and repose in a warm place until it has doubled in size, or for 30 minutes (whichever is first).

3 Line a high-sided baking tray with parchment paper. Use a scraper to turn the dough out of the bowl, then start to create buns by cutting it in half, still using the scraper. Carry on dividing until you have 16, ideally equal-ish pieces. In the palm of your hand, make the pieces firmly round so they will stand pert on the baking tray. Line 'em up 4 by 4 with a finger's space between each bun.

4 Cover the tin and leave in a toasty place until your buns have doubled in size, 30–50 minutes. Meanwhile, heat the oven (and baking stone, if you have one) to 210°C.

5 In a jug, whisk the crossing mix and pour it into a piping bag. (No lumps, please.) Deftly cross the buns by piping a lattice across the length and width of the tin.

6 Bake the buns. The very moment you have golden tops and bottoms, whip them out and immediately brush them with spicy bun wash.

7 Share your hot cross buns while still warm and spicy from the oven, slathered in butter that will yield into the soft, soft crumb with its plump fruit, and trickle down the wafer crust. Your home will fill with the aroma of Easter as you enjoy them with a cup of tea. Enormous reward for your care and toil, and a noble nod at a great baking tradition and the greatest story there has ever been.

ENRICHED DOUGHS

CHELSEA BUNS

1 You can use the dough recipe to make Chelsea buns as well. Make the dough (without the mixed spice and zest). After the dough has had its first rise, roll it out into a rectangle on a floured work surface. Once the dough is about 5mm thick and, as you face it, longer by half than it is wide, slather it with a wodge of melted butter save for a 2-inch (5cm) strip at the front edge – nothing goes on this except for a light brush of water. Then scatter the dried fruit and zest evenly over the buttered dough and sprinkle 10g ground cinnamon and 5g grated nutmeg on top. Roll the dough tightly towards you starting with the top edge. Once you've rolled a massive sweet sausage, brush this with more melted butter (it'll make them even more delicious and they'll be easier to separate later). Then take a very sharp knife and cut 4cm discs of bun dough spirals. Line a large roasting tin with baking parchment and place the buns in it, separated by only a small gap so that as they rise for the final time they rise upwards and together. Heat the oven (and baking stone) to 210°C. Once they have doubled in size, carefully place in the oven and bake until just golden on top and underneath. Before they cool, brush with Tom's spicy bun wash.

TEA CAKES

1 Use the hot cross bun recipe to make cracking tea cakes, replacing the mixed spice with 5g ground cinnamon and 5g grated nutmeg. After the first rise, divide the dough into 16 pieces and mould them into round rolls. Leave them to rest for a couple of minutes and then, on a floured surface, rolling-pin them out to a size just bigger than a lady's palm. Tray them up on baking parchment with a little space between each one, cover them and set to prove for a final time. Heat the oven (and baking stone) to 210°C. Once they have doubled in size, carefully place in the oven and bake until just golden on top and underneath, but still light in colour around the sides. Before they cool, brush with Tom's spicy bun wash. Split and toasted, with lots of butter, this has got afternoon snack wrapped up.

LUXURY GIANT HOT CROSS BUN

MAKES 1 BIG BUN

What better baking way of celebrating new life, spring and more bank holidays than you can shake a baguette at than with a giant hot cross bun!

FOR THE DOUGH:

500ml warm milk, plus a little extra if needed

a cigarillo of cinnamon

¼ nutmeg, grated

a pinch of saffron

½ dozen cloves

2 star anise

zest of 1 orange

480g strong white flour

5g sea salt

15g dried yeast (or 30g fresh yeast if you can get it)

100g caster sugar

100g soft butter

3 egg yolks, plus 1 extra yolk for glazing

150g raisins

finely grated zest of 1 lemon

FOR THE CROSSING MIX:

50g strong white flour, a pinch of salt, a pinch of sugar, a knob of butter and 50ml water

FOR THE BUN WASH:

1 eggcup of boiling water

2 tsp sugar

1 pinch of mixed spice

1 Simmer the milk and spices with the orange zest for 30 minutes until reduced by half. With a pestle, push the lot through a sieve into a mixing bowl. Add more milk if necessary until the liquid weighs 225g.

2 Weigh all the other ingredients, except the raisins and lemon zest, into the mixing bowl. With a firm hand, stir the lot together with wooden spoon. Turn the loose dough onto a bench and knead for a full 15 minutes until the dough is smooth and stretchy. Only add more flour or milk if you really have to. (You could do this in a mixer with a dough hook, with 10 minutes of kneading.)

3 Gently work in the raisins and lemon zest. Put the dough back into the mixing bowl, cover and rest in a warm place until it has doubled in size, or for 30 minutes (whichever is first).

4 Line a large high-sided baking tray with baking parchment. Firmly round the dough into a pert jumbo bun, place in the tray and brush with an egg yolk glaze. Cover the tin and leave in a toasty place until your giant bun has doubled in size, 30–50 minutes. Heat the oven (and baking stone) to 210°C.

5 In a jug, whisk your crossing mix and pour it into a piping bag. Cross your bun.

6 Bake the giant hot cross bun for 50 minutes – turning the oven temperature down to 180°C after 15 minutes – until you have a golden top and a well-baked bottom that rings hollow when tapped. Whip it out and immediately brush with the spicy bun wash.

ENRICHED DOUGHS

201

SPINACH ENGLISH MUFFINS

• MAKES 12 •

I love eggs Benedict, and my preference is to have it with ham, but I've often seen it offered florentine style (with spinach) and felt I might be missing out. Sooooo, I've tweaked the English muffin to include the spinach. This royal breakfast can now be enjoyed belt and braces style with the best of both dishes. Have cake and eat it for breakfast. Surely the best start to a great day.

30g butter	½ a nutmeg, grated (1 tsp)
10g sugar	200g fresh spinach, chopped
300ml milk	450g strong white flour
10g dried yeast (or 20g fresh yeast if you can get it)	pinch of sea salt
	cornmeal or semolina for dusting

1 Weigh the butter and sugar into a pan and melt them. Then add the milk, yeast and nutmeg. Warm the yeasty milk mix ever so gently, to tepid. No hotter or you could kill the yeast. Add the spinach and stir it all in.

2 Weigh the flour into a mixing bowl with the salt and add the wet mix. Work the lot into a very wet dough, before kneading it on a work surface for 15 minutes, or in a mixer with a dough hook for 10. Either way, mix, knead and develop the dough until it's soft, smooth and elastic. Cover the dough and put it back into the mixing bowl and leave for half an hour to rise.

3 Start warming a heavy non-stick pan on a low heat. Tip the very sticky dough out on to a work surface liberally covered with cornmeal or semolina, then dust the top quite generously. Gently stretch the dough out, attempting to get the depth as even as possible, until the thickness is about 2cm, or thereabouts. Using a round 3-inch (7.5cm) cutter, cut discs from the dough and carefully place them in the pan to dry fry. A sprinkle of cornmeal or semolina in the pan helps to stop the muffins from sticking. Fry them for 5 or more minutes, before carefully flipping over to fry through on the other side; a palette knife is useful for this. Keep an eye and nose out to see that they don't burn.

TOM'S TIPS

Always break open a muffin by hand or with a fork. This increases the surface area, ensuring it absorbs more of the luscious hollandaise. To make plain muffins, simply omit the spinach and nutmeg and reduce the flour by 100g. This will make about 8 muffins.

EGGS BENEDICT – POACHED EGG, HOLLANDAISE SAUCE, HAM, AND SPINACH MUFFINS

— FEEDS 4 —

I have strong memories of cooking this in my first kitchen job at Tom's café in Nailsworth when I was sixteen. Riding my moped to work, I would practise in my head how to make it, knowing that at least forty would be ordered that morning.

4 spinach muffins	pepper	1 tsp white wine vinegar
1 tsp white wine vinegar	**FOR THE HOLLANDAISE:**	salt
8 eggs	250g butter	1 lemon, halved
8 thin slices of ham	2 egg yolks	

1 To make the hollandaise, first melt the butter very gently in a saucepan. As the butter melts, skim off any foam that rises to the surface. This can be tossed through vegetables or incorporated into a mash, so put it aside for later use. In another pan, heat some water and place a metal bowl on top. Add the yolks and vinegar, and whisk in a pinch of salt. Keep whisking over the heat till the yolks start to thicken. This is called a sabayon. Reduce the heat and keep whisking.

2 Slowly trickle in the butter, whisking all the while. As the melted butter is whisked into the egg yolk it will start to thicken like a mayonnaise. Keep adding till all the butter is mixed in. You should have a fairly thick yellow sauce. Have a little taste and squeeze in some lemon juice. This slightly thins the sauce and freshens the flavour. Remove from the heat and cover to keep warm.

3 Bring a large pan of water to a gentle simmer and add the vinegar. Carefully break in the eggs and poach for 2 minutes, or until the whites are firm but the yolks still runny. Remove with a slotted spoon and drain off excess water.

4 Warm the muffins and break in half. Spread a little butter if you're feeling naughty. Lay a piece of ham on each half of the muffin. Place the eggs on the ham and spoon the hollandaise sauce over the lot. A twist of pepper is about all that is needed.

DOUGHNUTS

• MAKES 12–18 •

Who doesn't like a doughnut? Who didn't have lick-your-lips competitions as a child? Sugar-coated lips, jam dribbling down your chin, feeling slightly sick after you've scoffed your third one. If there is anything better than a doughnut, it's a home-made one.

FOR THE FIRST STAGE:	125g milk	**FOR THE THIRD STAGE:**
120ml water	250g plain flour	60g butter, cut into small pieces
8g dried yeast (or 16g fresh)	250g strong flour	
120g plain flour	90g sugar	1 litre oil, for frying
FOR THE SECOND STAGE:	10g salt	
8g dried yeast (or 16g fresh)	6 yolks	

1 In a mixer, beat the ingredients for the first stage together for 5 minutes, then cover and leave somewhere warm to rise. This will take an hour or so. This gets the dough working before the sugar is added, as too much sugar can kill the yeast.

2 For the second stage, beat these ingredients into the first dough. It needs to mix for 15 minutes till you have a soft dough. It will be quite tight.

3 For the third stage, slowly beat in the butter, bit by bit. If you add it too fast it won't mix in properly and the dough will turn out greasy. It will take about 5 minutes to mix in properly. Cover the dough and leave for 30 minutes to relax before portioning into balls.

4 On a clean surface, cut the dough into small balls, about 50g for small doughnuts or 80g for large ones. Roll the dough pieces in your hands to form smooth balls. Place on a tray and cover with a tea towel. These need to rise before being fried. In a warm place this will take about 45 minutes.

5 Heat a fat-fryer to 160°C (or warm up vegetable oil in a large saucepan using a probe to gauge the temperature accurately), gently place the doughnuts in the fryer using a slotted spoon, and fry for 2–5 minutes on one side. When brown, flip them over with the slotted spoon. If the balls are totally round they can be buggers to flip. Cook on the other side, again for 2–5 minutes until golden. Remove and drain briefly on kitchen paper. Then toss in caster sugar, and either fill or eat while warm. Suggested fillings: strawberry jam or other fruit jam, custard, flavoured custard, apple or other fruit compote.

HOMEMADE JAM

• MAKES 1KG (2 JARS) •

Our auntie makes some pretty awesome jam. Great if you have an excess of fruit and not at all difficult to do.

| 500g fresh strawberries | 500g jam sugar (this has pectin added) | juice of 1 lemon |

1 First, place a saucer in the freezer to chill. In a large, thick-based pan, add all the ingredients and bring to the boil, stirring. Turn down and simmer, keeping on stirring so as not to burn the bottom. The jam will take about 10–20 minutes to reach setting point. To test, drop a small dribble onto the cold saucer. When it cools, run your finger through it. If the sides hold up like a jelly, then it is ready; if not, it needs a little longer. When done, leave for 15 minutes to cool slightly and start to set.

2 Take a couple of clean jam jars and place in a hot oven for 5 minutes to sterilise. Quickly divide the jam between the jars and screw the lids on. These will keep for 6 months, easily.

HENRY'S TIPS

Try a different fruit – raspberries, gooseberries, blackberries and plums all make excellent jams. To fill a doughnut, put the jam in a piping bag, poke inside the doughnut and squeeze until it will take no more.

CUSTARD

· FOR 12–18 DOUGHNUTS ·

Custard doughnuts might be my favourite of all, big mouthfuls of crispy sweet dough with an exploding centre that slides down your chin in the best way possible. I personally like vanilla custard, but those of you who like chocolate or other flavours, feel free to experiment.

3 large egg yolks	20g cornflour	½ tablespoon liqueur: Grand Marnier, brandy, kirsch (optional)
50g granulated white sugar	300ml whole milk	
20g plain flour	½ vanilla pod, split lengthways	

1 In a round-based bowl, whisk the yolks and the sugar together, sift in the flours and beat until smooth. Don't leave eggs and sugar together unwhisked as the sugar will cook the yolks and leave you with spots of solid yolk in the custard.

2 In a thick-based saucepan, bring the milk and vanilla to the boil. Remove from the heat and, while whisking slowly, pour into the bowl. Keep whisking till you have a smooth mixture. Pour it all back into the pan, use a spatula to scrape all the seeds off the bottom.

3 Place back on the heat and bring to the boil, stirring all the time. As the custard boils the mixture will thicken. Keep boiling and stirring for 3 minutes to cook out the raw flour flavour, then remove from the heat and, if using, stir in the booze. Pour through a fine sieve into a flat container. Place in the fridge to chill.

4 When cold, give it a quick mix to smooth the custard, scoop into a piping bag, ram inside the warm doughnut and split its edges.

5 For a lighter pastry cream, fold in 120ml softly whipped cream to the cooled custard.

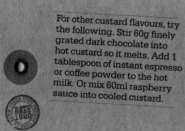

For other custard flavours, try the following. Stir 60g finely grated dark chocolate into hot custard so it melts. Add 1 tablespoon of instant espresso or coffee powder to the hot milk. Or mix 60ml raspberry sauce into cooled custard.

HENRY'S TIPS

TOM'S LONG STICKY DIPPY STICKS

MAKES 10 STICKS WITH PLENTY OF DUNKING

So quick are these doughnuts to make, you might start a habit that's hard to break. They are like sparkled crispy twigs, standing to attention, ready to plunge into a chocolate lagoon. The name is also a nod to 'Tom Long', a highwayman who was hanged close to where we now live; the gallows post is still there.

400ml water	oil for frying	100ml double cream
30ml oil	caster sugar for dredging	75ml Guinness or other stout
260g self-raising flour	**FOR THE CHOCOLATE DUNKING SAUCE:**	small knob of butter
pinch of salt	100g dark chocolate	pinch of salt
20g sugar	10g sugar	

1 First, make the sauce. Gently heat all the ingredients in a small pan, stirring till the butter and chocolate have melted and the sauce is smooth and glossy. Don't have too much heat or the chocolate and cream will split. Also, any remaining Guinness is best enjoyed during the making of the doughnut sticks. If you don't fancy Guinness, then milk is an acceptable alternative.

2 For the doughnut sticks, bring the water and oil to the boil in a saucepan. With the remaining dry ingredients in a bowl, slowly pour in the hot liquid, using a quick fork action to mix. Don't overmix: you should have a stiff sticky dough.

3 Heat a fat-fryer to 170°C (or warm up vegetable oil in a pan using a probe to gauge the temperature accurately). Either place the mix into a piping bag, or quickly, with light hands, roll into longish sticks. Place a few at a time in the fryer, using a slotted spoon. They should take about 3–5 minutes to cook till they are golden and crispy on the outside and fluffy in the middle. Remove, drain excess oil off and toss in caster sugar. Caution, wait at least 30 seconds, or they will burn your lips.

4 Dip the sticky sticks and devour.

THINGS MEN LIKE TO MAKE

CLASSIC DISHES AND CELEBRATION FOOD

Throughout this book and especially in this chapter are many of my favourite recipes, dishes I cook over and over again. They are solid, reliable recipes and I'm sure you can't go wrong. If you want, follow the ingredients exactly. But I'd encourage you to go off-piste from time to time. Follow your whim. Bring in a change or two. It's the way to learn. By experimenting, you build confidence, and that can only be a good thing. Just remember to cook in season. The produce not only tastes better but is usually better value. Happily, it's often what your heart wants anyway. In winter I crave parsnips but in summer I want courgettes. I was lucky enough to work with very fine chefs when I was in London, who taught me how to appreciate produce and to cook from the heart. Cooking is subjective. Relax and trust your eye and your tastebuds. After all, you're the one eating it. Most of all, just get in there and do it. Growing up in a bakery, with four hungry brothers and a sister, it was always all about food. Now I run the Hobbs House butchery, and I still cook whenever I can. What I cook depends on how I feel, and this, I think, is the best starting point – because more than anything, I'm really just someone who likes to eat.

Henry

THE FULL ENGLISH

Tom and I were having a debate about what makes the best English breakfast. He said he likes his baked in the oven. For me, that's not a fried breakfast. I suspect he likes his with a poached egg. For me, if you're going to have a Full English it's got to include a frying pan at some point, with minimal pan washing between stages so all those lovely bacon flavours end up in the sauce of the beans, with just a quick spruce at the end and then a proper fried egg, sunny-side-up every time. Everyone has their favourite combo. Overleaf you'll find mine.

HENRY'S FULL ENGLISH

━━━━ • FEEDS 2 • ━━━━

A breakfast without pork would be a sad situation indeed. If I was allowed, I would eat bacon every morning. However, I hold out and go for it every Sunday. I dream of Sunday mornings when I can awake at my leisure and gorge on a proper breakfast. A man's breakfast, the sort of food upon which battles were won. For that brief moment I feel like a king, lord of my castle.

oil for frying	2 slices of white bread	4 eggs
4 chipolatas	2 large mushrooms	**CONDIMENTS:**
4 rashers of dry-cure bacon	knob of butter	HP, ketchup, mustard
2 thick slices of black pudding	1 tin of beans	2 mugs of tea

1 Heat the oven to 120°C. This is just to keep the breakfast warm while other bits are cooking. Heat a large frying pan and add a splash of oil. Add the chipolatas and gently brown on all sides. Rule number one with sausages is that you cook them gently, otherwise they burst. When they are coloured but still raw, add the bacon and black pudding. This part of proceedings will take about 10 minutes. I like my bacon crispy but not completely obliterated.

2 Remove the sausages, black pudding and bacon to a warm plate and leave in the oven. Add another splash of oil to the used pan and fry the bread slices on both sides for 2 minutes till golden and crispy and the bacon fat has seeped into the bread. I love fried bread, but my wife is more of a wholemeal sourdough kind, so this is for when she is away. Remove and keep warm.

3 Slice the mushrooms into chunks, heat a knob of butter and fry them in the pan. When they are coloured, season generously and toss around. If you were feeling cheffy, a sprig of thyme would be nice here, but not strictly authentic. Set aside. Pour the beans into the pan and heat whilst scraping up all the crispy bits so you get those lovely porky flavours into the sauce. When bubbling, scrape into a bowl and keep warm. Give the pan a quick rinse and heat again with some oil. Crack the eggs in. You want it to be hot enough that the white starts to bubble but not colour too much. Season the top and cook for about 2 minutes till the white has set but the yolk is molten. Start to plate up just before the eggs are cooked. Attack with great haste, washed down with mugs of tea.

TOM'S FULL ENGLISH

• FEEDS MANY •

My absolute favourite meal in the world is when the weekend is ours, great friends or siblings have stayed over, and the house is filled with the aromatic wake-up call of breakfast and coffee.

1 Give your sausages a head start by putting them in a roasting tin and sticking them in a hot oven. After 10 minutes, add some big mushrooms (portobello or field), and next to these some halved seasoned tomatoes or cherry vine tomatoes. Over the top lay rashers of bacon.

2 Add thick slices of black pudding too. Eggs are to be cooked on the side, scrambled, fried or poached. Serve with lashings of buttered toast, a big pot of freshly ground coffee and a crate of oranges for squeezing. Dive in. For the next hour, it's breakfast time.

TOM'S TIPS

Pour some of the breakfast gravy over the top and soak the rest up from the pan tray with bread. Yum.

MARMALADE

MAKES PLENTY: 4 JARS

My auntie Tory is a bit of a preserve whiz. I enjoy a marmalade-making session in January when Seville oranges are at their height. I make enough to last the year and inevitably it's more than I need but it makes for nice presents.

4 Seville oranges

1.3kg caster sugar

1 Cut a few slits in the oranges and put in a large pan. Cover with 2 litres of water and bring to a simmer, then drain the water and add fresh. This takes some of the bitterness out. Bring to a simmer again, put the lid on and cook until the oranges are soft and tender: about 25 minutes.

2 Strain the oranges – reserving the water they boiled in – and leave them to cool a little; the insides can be outrageously hot at this point. When cool enough to handle, cut them open to allow the steam to flow out. Then scoop out the seeds and pulp: this is where the pectin comes from that makes the marmalade set. Tie into a muslin cloth or similar, place back into the pan and pour in 1.5 litres of the reserved orange water. Stir in the sugar and bring to the boil. Place a small plate in the freezer. This is for later use. The marmalade will take about 30 minutes to get to setting point. Stir frequently so it doesn't catch on the bottom.

3 Meanwhile, either chop the orange peel into thin strips or blitz quickly in a food processor. Set to one side. You want to stir these in about 5 minutes before the end. To judge this, take the plate out of the freezer and dribble a teaspoon of marmalade on to it. When it cools, run your finger through. If the sides hold up like a jelly, then it is ready; if not, it needs a little longer. Remove from the heat and leave to stand for 15 minutes before pouring into sterilised jars. This stops the orange pieces from floating to the top. The marmalade will last for 1 year, no problem.

Try using lemon or grapefruit if you fancy a change. Marmalade goes great with Cheddar on sourdough toast. It does what pickle does, only better. Whereas vinegar can overpower a cheese, marmalade has a bitter-sweet quality that makes a perfect partnership. A brilliant breakfast, for when the Full English would be too much.

HENRY'S TIPS

THINGS MEN LIKE TO MAKE

CASSOULET

• FEEDS 2 •

Never plan to do much after eating a cassoulet. Nothing more than a prolonged stint on the sofa. This dish makes me very happy indeed.

2 confit duck legs	40g duck fat	400g tin of cooked haricot beans
4 Toulouse sausages	½ chilli	salt and pepper
1 onion	small bunch of thyme	1 tsp sherry vinegar
4 garlic cloves	400g tin of tomatoes	handful of breadcrumbs
50g pancetta	300ml chicken stock	

1 Heat the oven to 150°C. Put the confit duck legs and the sausages in a shallow flameproof casserole dish and place in the oven for 20 minutes to brown. Take out and put the sausage and duck to one side. Don't wash the dish: all those loverly crispy bits are gold. Chop the onion, garlic and pancetta.

2 Heat the duck fat in the casserole dish, and gently brown the onion, garlic and pancetta. Chop the chilli and strip the leaves from the thyme, then add to the casserole dish with the tomatoes and chicken stock. Bring to the boil and simmer for 15 minutes. Add the beans, season with salt and pepper and add the sherry vinegar.

3 Turn the heat down, and carefully nestle the duck and sausages in. Sprinkle with the breadcrumbs and finish in the oven for 1 hour until crisply topped, and the aroma of garlicky duck fills the room.

Double the quantities and make cassoulet for a group: this means cooking it more slowly, which gives the beans more time to soak up the flavours and form just the most amazing crust. Or make double so you have leftovers, such as for wicked beans on toast (see page 150).

HENRY'S TIPS

THINGS MEN LIKE TO MAKE

FISH STEW WITH CROUTONS AND AIOLI

• FEEDS 4 •

I made this soup when I was eighteen, for eighty guests at my mother's fiftieth birthday, on an Aga that lost all its heat so the cooking had to be finished off on camping stoves. It remains one of my all-time comfort dishes. If I see fish soup on a menu, and I trust the kitchen, I can't turn it down.

12 shell-on prawns	1 fennel bulb, sliced	1 litre fish stock
20ml extra virgin olive oil	1 carrot, sliced	pinch of saffron
1 onion, finely diced	200ml dry white wine	salt and pepper
1 gurnard, filleted and pin-boned (but keep the bones), or other firm white fish	400g tin of tomatoes	1 lemon, optional
	herbs to taste: bay, fresh tarragon, fresh parsley	500g mussels
4 garlic cloves, crushed	grated zest of 1 orange	1 tsp each of finely chopped fresh parsley, tarragon, dill

1 Peel the prawns and set the meat aside. Heat a deep pan, add the oil and lightly brown the prawn shells and onion. Then add the gurnard bones, garlic, fennel and carrot, and fry for 10 minutes over a medium heat, till the vegetables soften. Turn the heat up and pour in the wine. Cook until reduced by about half, and scrape up any bits stuck to the bottom. Add the tomatoes, herbs and orange zest. Bring to the boil and add the fish stock. Simmer for 45 minutes. This will give you a wonderful base for your soup.

2 Pour through a fine sieve into a clean pan. Bring to the boil, add the saffron and season to taste. Squeeze some lemon in if you feel the flavour needs freshening up. Cut the gurnard fillets into small chunks. Add to the soup with the mussels and prawns and simmer for 3 minutes, or until the mussels open. Sprinkle in the fresh herbs and serve.

3 To make aioli, crush 2 garlic cloves to a smooth paste. Put in a round-based bowl with 2 egg yolks and the juice of half a lemon, and whisk well. Measure 50ml extra virgin olive oil and 50ml other vegetable oil into a jug. Whisking all the while, slowly add the oils, allowing the mixture to thicken gradually. When all the oil is added, you should have a stiff mayonnaise with a garlic kick. Season to taste and spoon into the hot soup.

4 To make croutons, use any white or sourdough bread. Cut off the crusts, rub the bread with a split garlic clove, then dice up into small cubes – I like them to be under 1cm in size – sprinkle with salt and pepper and fry in a little olive oil over a low heat. Keep turning them until they are crispy and firm. They do need to be good and firm, or they will go soggy in the soup.

THINGS MEN LIKE TO MAKE

ROAST LEG OF LAMB WITH BAKER'S POTATOES

⸺ FEEDS 8 ⸺

The combination of lamb, garlic, rosemary and anchovies is nothing new, but it's so good. Baked on top of a potato and onion gratin and you're knocking on heaven's door. I always opt for the English translation, being a baker 'born and bread', but it's very much the same recipe as the one that goes under a French name (boulangère). The juices from the lamb soak into the spuds: a wonderful dish.

1 leg of lamb, top bone ('h' bone) removed, with the shank bone left in	large sprig of rosemary, chopped	2 garlic cloves
	30ml extra virgin olive oil	100g butter
	salt and pepper	8 large Maris Piper potatoes
3 garlic cloves, sliced	**FOR THE BAKER'S POTATOES:**	500ml chicken stock
3 anchovy fillets, chopped	3 large onions	

1 Heat the oven to 200°C. Mix the garlic, anchovy, rosemary and olive oil together. Rub all over the lamb, inside and out, and season all over with salt and pepper. Tie the lamb up with some string and set aside until later.

2 Slice the onions and garlic. In a saucepan, melt 75g of the butter and slowly cook the onions and garlic till they are soft and slightly golden. Season and set aside.

3 Peel and slice the potatoes as thinly as possible. Don't be tempted to wash the potatoes at this stage; you need the starch on them to give the dish a good structure. Take a largish baking tray and scatter a layer of potatoes on the bottom, then a layer of onions. Season and then repeat the process. Keep going until you finish with a pretty, overlapping layer of potatoes in the fashion of fish scales. Place the leg of lamb on top and put into the oven for 30 minutes to brown off. When the leg has a beautiful golden colour, turn the heat down to 180°C. I like my lamb to be medium, slightly pink but with the fat well rendered. It will take about a further hour. To be totally accurate, use a temperature probe: 60°C internal temperature is perfect. Remove the lamb and wrap in tin foil to rest for at least 25 minutes.

4 Whack the heat up to 220°C and dot the remaining butter over the potatoes. They should be cooked by now so this is to brown and crisp the top. It will take roughly 20 minutes, but keep an eye on them and remove when ready.

5 Slice the lamb thinly and serve with the baker's potatoes.

BEEF WELLINGTON
• FEEDS 6 •

Few are they who don't get excited about this dish. Ruby-red beef fillet with earthy mushrooms and indulgent foie gras in a shield of crisp puff pastry. Done well, it can be mind-blowing. Leave out the foie gras if you think it's too much. (I wouldn't.)

1kg piece of the best beef fillet you can find	1 sprig of thyme	200g foie gras (optional)
salt and pepper	200g wild mushrooms, cleaned	500g block of all-butter puff pastry
20g butter	1 tsp truffle oil	
1 garlic clove	small pinch of chopped parsley	1 egg, to glaze
	1 Savoy cabbage	

1 Season the fillet liberally. Heat a large pan and, when hot, quickly brown the beef on all sides. Remove from the pan, put on a plate, allow to cool then put into the fridge to chill.

2 Melt the butter in a small pan. Crush the garlic and add to the pan with the thyme. Finely chop the mushrooms, add to the pan and fry until lightly browned and most of the moisture has been driven off, then season and stir in the truffle oil and parsley. Set aside to chill.

3 Pull off the large outer leaves of the cabbage and cut out the thick middle stem. Blanch in boiling water for 2 minutes, then remove and plunge into cold water. Drain, squeeze out excess moisture and lay them out on the worktop, overlapping, so they are big enough to wrap the fillet. Spread the mushrooms over the middle. Slice the foie gras, if using, and lay on top. Finally put the fillet on top and wrap the leaves round it. Make sure there are no gaps (this helps keep the juices away from the pastry). Place in the fridge to firm up.

4 Roll the pastry into a rectangle large enough to cover the whole fillet. Place the cabbage-wrapped fillet in the middle and wrap one side of the pastry right over so it meets the other side. Crimp the edges all round. Place in the fridge for at least 20 minutes to set the pastry. Then beat an egg with a pinch of salt and brush all over the Wellington to glaze it.

5 Heat the oven to 200°C. Heat a large baking tray to hot, then place the Wellington directly on it. This stops it getting a soggy butt. The pastry will take about 30 minutes to cook. To serve the beef rare will take about 40 minutes, so turn the oven down to 180°C after 20 minutes so the pastry doesn't burn. If you like it well done, add 20 minutes to the cooking time. Remove and rest the Wellington for 15 minutes somewhere warm. Slice and serve.

MASSIVE PORK PIE

• FEEDS AN ARMY FOR A WEEK •

This hugest of all pies was a regular feature on my menus when I first cooked in London with my friend Ant. We knew it was the right size when it dwarfed a pint glass. This may take some time to make, but it's a show-stopper. I made one for my wife's friend's birthday to show off and, boy, were they impressed. Hot water crust is possibly the easiest of all pastries; I feel the time has come for this overlooked pastry to shine in our kitchens once again.

	FOR THE JELLY STOCK:	FOR THE HOT WATER CRUST:
2kg pork shoulder, boned and rindless, coarsely minced	1 litre water	1 kg plain flour
500g bacon offcuts, chopped	2 pig's trotters	big pinch of salt
30g sage, chopped	1 onion and 1 carrot, roughly chopped	4 eggs
30ml Worcestershire sauce		400ml water
2 tbsp mace	herbs: a sprig of thyme and a bay leaf	320g lard (for home-rendered, see page 195)
2 big pinches cayenne		
salt and pepper	salt and peppercorns	1 egg, beaten, to glaze

1 In a saucepan, simmer the jelly ingredients for 3 hours. The jelly stock can be simmering while the pie is cooking. Heat the oven to 160°C. Mix all the pie ingredients together. (The bacon helps the pie to keep its colour.)

2 Make the hot water crust: mix the flour, salt and eggs together in a large bowl. Bring the water and lard to the boil, pour quickly into the flour and beat until it forms a smooth ball. Leave the pastry to cool for 5 minutes so you can handle it, then set a lump of pastry aside to make the lid. Using your fingers, press the rest of the pastry into a large, spring-release cake tin (about 23cm) and raise it up the sides before it cools and hardens. You want a little overhang at the top to fix the lid to. You have about 10 minutes to do this. Then fill the pie with the filling and top with a rolled-out lid in which you've cut a small round hole. Use any leftover pastry to make decorations. Crimp the edges.

3 Bake the pie for 2–3 hours. If it starts to brown too quickly, cover with some foil. The pie is cooked when it starts bubbling at the edges. Remove the pie from the oven and set aside for 30 minutes, then carefully release from the tin. Beat an egg and brush the pie all over. Return to the oven for 15 minutes to get a good golden hue.

4 Take the pie out of the oven again and let it cool a little so any tiny crevices seal themselves up. Then pour the hot jelly stock through the hole in the top, using a syringe or funnel. Leave the pie for 24 hours before eating.

PICCALILLI

MAKES 2 BIG JARS

The perfect partner to a pork pie. Make it at the height of summer, when the vegetables are at their best, and make a lot, as it lasts.

1kg total weight of vegetables: 1 large cauliflower, 3 onions, 1 large cucumber	30g cornflour	200g sugar
	20g mustard powder	600ml white wine vinegar
	20g turmeric	
50g sea salt	pinch of cayenne pepper	

1 Cut the cauliflower into small florets. I personally don't like the stalk, but use it if you would otherwise feel wasteful. Dice the onions. Split the cucumber lengthways and remove the seeds, then dice it nice and small. Place it all in a large bowl and mix in the salt. Cover and keep in the fridge for 24 hours. This draws the moisture out of the vegetables, helping to keep them nice and crunchy when pickled.

2 The next day, put the dry ingredients in a saucepan, whisk in the vinegar, then bring to the boil, stirring all the time. When it has thickened and is smooth and glossy, pour through a fine sieve into a bowl.

3 Take the vegetables from the fridge and wash well in plenty of water to get rid of excess salt. Stir the vegetables through the spicy paste. The result should be bright yellow in colour. Pour into sterilised jars and seal immediately. Use after 4 weeks. It will keep well for a year.

HENRY'S TIPS

Piccalilli is so much better if you take the time to cut the vegetables into evenly sized small chunks.

GOOSEBERRY AND ELDERFLOWER PIES
MAKES 4 SMALL PIES

This is a sweet take on a traditional pork pie. It will surprise your friends when they bite into the pie expecting savoury pork, finding delicious gooseberries instead.

FOR THE GOOSEBERRY FILLING:

100g fresh gooseberries

50g sugar

4 leaves gelatine

100ml elderflower juice

FOR THE HOT WATER CRUST:

175g lard (home-rendered Old Spot lard, if you can: see page 195)

200g water

500g plain flour

100g sugar

1 egg, beaten, to glaze

FOR THE CUSTARD:

100ml double cream

100ml milk

2 egg yolks

30g sugar

1 First prepare the gooseberry filling. Top and tail the little orbs and put into a pan with the sugar. Very briefly soften on a gentle flame until the gooseberries are barely giving. Soak the gelatine in cold water for a few minutes, allowing it to swell, then drain and squeeze out. Put in a pan, add the elderflower juice and warm a little to melt the gelatine. Set aside.

2 For the pastry, heat the lard with the water until melted. Take four small pie moulds (or ramekins or dariole moulds), brush with a little lard and dust with some flour. Put the flour and sugar in a bowl, pour in the hot lard and beat vigorously with a wooden spoon. Take a nugget of pastry and put in a pie mould. Using your fingers, build the pastry up the mould sides. When the top has been reached with a little overhang, loosely spoon some of the gooseberries into the mould, then top up with the elderflower jelly. Roll a separate piece of pastry and place

on top. Crimp the two parts together and trim off any excess. Repeat for the rest.

3 Heat the oven to 200°C. Bake the pies for 15 minutes, until the pastry starts to colour. Allow to cool a little, then turn out of the cases and brush all over with the beaten egg. Turn the oven up to 230°C. Return the pies to the oven and cook for 5 minutes, to make them shiny. Take out, cool, then chill in the fridge until the jelly has set.

4 To make the custard, heat the cream and milk to a gentle simmer. Meanwhile, in a round-bottomed bowl, whisk the yolks and sugar until fairly pale, about 3 minutes. Take a ladle of boiled cream and whisk into the yolk mixture. Then pour the whole lot back into the pan and, on a very low heat, start to cook the custard. It will thicken as the egg yolks cook. The custard is done when it coats the back of a spoon.

5 Serve the pies on small plates with the custard in a jug. Delicious.

STEAMED DATE AND WALNUT PUDDING

· FEEDS 6 ·

This pudding is based on Sodbury cake, a heritage recipe of ours, one we've made for generations in the bakery. We were approached a few years ago by Highgrove, Prince Charles's residence, asking for the recipe for a book they were doing. Apparently it was the Queen Mother's favourite, and whenever she came to Highgrove, which is not far from our bakery, she requested it. It was our old family favourite for decades, and now we know it was the Queen Mother's too. We were totally chuffed to be asked – but we didn't give them the recipe. This recipe isn't for Sodbury cake, but it's pretty damned close. And as a pudding, it's better. Sasha Jenner, Hobbs House original patisserie chef, came up with this version.

butter for greasing	50g dark molasses	pinch of salt
175g self-raising flour	100g dates, chopped	1 egg
75g vegetable suet	100g walnuts, chopped	150ml milk
2 tbsp sugar	zest of 1 lemon	

1 Butter a 1½-pint pudding bowl. Put all the ingredients except the egg and the milk in a mixing bowl and mix together well. Beat the egg into the milk in a jug, then stir into the cake mixture. The result should be of a loose, dropping consistency. Pour it into the pudding bowl.

2 Cut a disc of greaseproof paper large enough to fit the top of the pudding, then cut a second, larger disc and put that, with a pleat in it, right over the top so it overhangs the sides. Tie it in place with kitchen string, place in a large pan and pour in boiling water until it comes just over halfway up the sides of the bowl. If you tie the string around the pudding and over the top to make a handle, you've got a convenient way to get the hot pudding out.

3 Bring to the boil and simmer for 2½ hours. Check periodically that it has not boiled dry. Invert on to a large plate to serve.

Sticky toffee sauce is very good with this. Put the following in a small saucepan: 80g butter, 1 tablespoon of soft brown sugar and 1 tablespoon of molasses, 2 tablespoons of double cream, the zest of 1 lemon and a shot of whisky, brandy or Armagnac. Bring to the boil, stirring. Pour over the pudding just before serving, and scatter with chopped walnuts.

TOM'S TIPS

ESTD 1920

'GET OUT OF TROUBLE' CHOCOLATE CAKE

——— MAKES 1 BIG CAKE ———

I make this for my wife, Jess, and it's won me many brownie points. Most women love chocolate, and I truly believe that every man should have a chocolate recipe or two up his sleeve to pull out in time of need. This recipe is versatile: it can be made large for a kick-ass birthday cake, or you can cook it in individual pots and serve it as a delicious dessert after an anniversary meal. I have my friend Rosie Sykes to thank for it.

250g butter	250g sugar	10 whites
500g good chocolate (70%)	10 yolks	cream, to serve

1 Over a gentle flame, heat a pan of water. Place the butter and chocolate in a metal bowl and cover with cling film, place on the pan and let the steam melt the chocolate. It's important not to stir the mixture or let any moisture get into the chocolate or it may 'seize' and go grainy. Take off the heat when done and pull off the cling film.

2 In an electric mixer, beat the sugar and yolks till they are pale and fluffy, about 10 minutes. On a slow speed, pour in the melted chocolate and butter, and beat until smooth and glossy.

3 Whisk the egg whites to stiff peaks; it's easier done in a mixer if you're not feeling hard-core. Using a metal spoon, gently fold the egg whites into the cake mixture. Add the whites in two stages: this keeps the mixture light and fluffy. Don't overmix or the air will be lost.

4 Heat the oven to 180°C and grease a 30cm tin. Spoon the mixture into the tin and bake for 30–40 minutes, depending on how done you want it. I always like a slightly gooey centre. Leave to rest, then serve while still warm, with cream.

The same recipe makes a really tasty soufflé-style pudding, enough for 12. Grease 12 small pots, and spoon the mixture in. I like to add a few raspberries in the bottom, or a compote of stewed prunes in a boozy syrup. Bake at 180°C for 9 minutes. The top will slightly rise up but the centre will be runny and delicious.

HENRY'S TIPS

APPLE CRUMBLE WITH VANILLA ICE CREAM

· FEEDS 6 TO 8 ·

Nothing quite beats a huge bowl of steaming crumble to warm the bones on a chilly winter night. Using apples scrumped from a tree whilst on a windy walk is the best way to start a crumble. I make this at least ten times a year. Cold crumble eaten straight out of the fridge the next day is one of life's treats.

	FOR THE CRUMBLE:	**TO FINISH AND SERVE:**
4 large Bramley apples, or whatever you have found	200g butter, diced	50g flaked almonds
50g butter	200g ground almonds	1 tub of quality vanilla ice cream (Marshfield or Winstones, if you are round our way) or custard (see page 234), to serve
100g brown sugar	200g brown sugar	
grated zest of 1 lemon	200g flour	

1 Peel and dice the apples. Heat a large pan and melt the butter. As soon as it starts to foam, add the apple and fry quickly. Add the sugar and lemon zest. Turn the heat down and cook for 10 minutes or until the apple is soft and giving with just a little bite. Pour into an oven dish.

2 In a large bowl, rub the butter into the ground almonds, sugar and flour. When it is like breadcrumbs, spread evenly on top of the apples.

3 Heat the oven to 180°C. Bake the crumble for 40 minutes. When it is golden and bubbling, scatter on the flaked almonds and give it 5 more minutes.

4 Remove from the oven and serve while still hot with the ice cream or custard.

Add blackberries or other scrumped fruit to the apple for extra delight.

HENRY'S TIPS

ESTD 1920

EASTER BISCUITS

MAKES 12–16 BISCUITS

Seek out the rare oil of cassia. Its unique and distinctive aroma wafts around the Hobbs House bakery shops in the weeks before Easter, tempting people in. Misused, it can strip paint, or embalm a body, but just the right tiny amount is a fine thing in a buttery and short biscuit. Enjoy with a good cup of tea, or strong coffee, but definitely with a friend, and savour the spice whilst scheming for summer.

100g organic golden caster sugar	250g plain flour	2 tbsp milk
	½ tsp baking powder	80g currants
100g soft butter	tiniest drop of oil of cassia or 1 tsp of mixed spice	caster sugar
1 organic egg		

1 Beat the sugar and butter together until it's soft and fluffy. Plop the egg on top and whip her till she's all in. Fold in the flour, baking powder and the oil of cassia or spice. How much oil of cassia you use depends on your taste but also on how strong the one you've got is. It should come in a small bottle that only dispenses a drop at a time. Anything from 1 to 5 drops could be good. Gently mix the lot together while adding the milk – tweak your quota to yield a roll-out-able dough. Lastly knead in the currants.

2 Heat the oven to 200°C. Put parchment paper on a big baking tray.

3 On a floured table, roll out the dough to the thickness of a bunny rabbit's ear (5mm). Stamp out Easter biscuits with a pretty round fluted cutter and lay on the tray.

4 Bake until the edges just start to golden and they have the tiniest bit of colour underneath (about 12 minutes), then remove immediately. Allow to cool on the tray and sprinkle with caster sugar while still hot.

Cool on the tray so the biscuits can continue to bake as they cool down. This way you can easily achieve the perfect bake. However, if you've overbaked them, slide off the tray immediately.

TOM'S TIPS

BUTTERMILK PUDDING

— • MAKES 6 • —

Similar to pannacotta, but so much better; the buttermilk gives it the edge. Really good with Easter biscuits and some poached fruit. See page 166 for home-made buttermilk.

200ml milk	100g sugar	300ml buttermilk
200ml double cream	5 small gelatine leaves	splash of lemon juice
½ vanilla pod, split lengthways	(⅓ pack weighing 25g)	

1 In a large pan, heat the milk, cream and vanilla. When near boiling, remove from the heat and leave to infuse.

2 Fill a bowl with cold water and, leaf by leaf, add the gelatine to soften it. Leave for 5 minutes, then remove and squeeze out the excess water.

3 When the milk has cooled slightly, remove the vanilla pod and stir in the sugar, followed by the gelatine. (If the gelatine goes in when the liquid is too hot, its setting properties can be affected; too cold and it won't melt properly.) When the mixture is cooler still – at about room temperature – stir in the buttermilk and lemon juice. Buttermilk splits really easily so it must be cool when added.

4 Divide the mixture into 6 small moulds (about 125ml), place in the fridge and leave overnight to set. They will last for 5 days, but are at their best eaten the next day.

5 To unmould, take the moulds from the fridge, dip the base in a little hot water for 10 seconds, turn over and release on to a plate. Give the plate a little shake and watch with joy as the orbs wobble.

Poached forced rhubarb is my favourite accompaniment. Gooseberries stewed in a little elderflower syrup are also delicious. Poached summer apricots with a little ginger root also works a treat. The puddings last for 5 days in the fridge but get quite solid. For mega wobble, they are best fresh.

HENRY'S TIPS

FRUIT CAKE

— MAKES 1 CAKE —

My favourite fruit cake at Easter and Christmas. At Easter-time, simply put a layer of marzipan in the middle and eleven Faithful Apostles balls of marzipan on top. For Christmas, finish off with the traditional enrobing of marzipan and decorate with icing in family style. You can never have too much fruit cake, in my opinion.

FOR THE CAKE:

125g soft butter

125g organic soft brown sugar

3 small organic eggs

170g white flour

a big three-fingered pinch of baking powder (3g)

a big three-fingered pinch of mixed spice (3g)

a small pinch of ground cinnamon

2 tbsp black treacle (Christmas cake) or 1 tbsp golden syrup (Simnel)

125g chopped almonds (Christmas cake)

1 shot of brandy (Christmas only)

FOR THE FRUIT:

125g sultanas

125g currants

125g glacé cherries

the chopped peel of 1 lemon and 1 orange

50g mixed candied peel (Christmas only)

150ml brandy (Christmas only)

TO FINISH:

400g marzipan

apricot jam, 1 beaten egg

FOR CHRISTMAS:

bottle of brandy

either 500g fondant icing or, for royal icing, 500g icing sugar, 2 egg whites and lemon juice

FOR AN EASTER SIMNEL CAKE

1 Heat the oven to 150°C. Line and grease a 20cm round cake tin.

2 Beat the butter and sugar until it's softer and fluffier than an Easter bunny. Slowly mix in the eggs whilst whipping at tremendous speed. Once the eggs are all in, you can cast the next group of ingredients into the mix and beat thoroughly so the batter you have is lumpless. Then gradually stir in all the fruit.

3 Plop half the mixture into the tin and level it off. Cover this with a 150g disc of marzipan, rolled out to the thickness of a little finger. On top of this goes the rest of the rich cake mix. Smooth it down with a slight dip in the middle, which will allow for the cake to rise without resulting in a bulge in the centre.

4 Bake the cake for one and a half hours, or until you can clean-skewer her. Oust the cake from its tin and cool on a wire rack. Once the cake has cooled, you can brush the top with apricot jam: the confectioner's anti-bacterial guerrilla glue.

5 Roll two-thirds of the remaining marzipan out so it can cover the top of the cake. Make 11 Faithful Apostles balls with the last of the marzipan and set them around the circumference. Paint the almondy decoration with the beaten egg. Under a hot grill or with a blow torch, lightly singe the uppermost bits of the cake.

FOR CHRISTMAS CAKE

1 Set your phone reminder alarm to bleep in early October. Start with the fruit. At the first opportunity, weigh the fruit into a bowl and pour over the brandy, cover and leave to soak for a day. Make the cake as shown on page 244 (for the measure against which to judge the fluffiness of your butter and sugar mixture, consider Father Christmas's beard) and bake it without the marzipan inner layer – you need all the marzipan for the ceremonial enrobing.

2 When the cake has cooled, feed it with brandy and wrap tightly in baking paper. Store in an airtight tin. Every week or so, turn the cake upside down, skewer the base several times and pour about 2 teaspoons of brandy onto it, let it soak in, then return the cake to the paper and store in the tin.

3 A week before Christmas, or whenever tickles your festive fancy, get the boozy cake out from its intoxicating tin and brush all over with apricot jam. Roll the marzipan out so it can cover the entire cake. Then, cover the cake.

4 On a flat work surface covered with a light sprinkling of icing sugar, roll out the fondant icing, if using, and cover the cake. Make sure there are no air pockets under either the marzipan or icing.

5 For the royal icing option, whisk 2 egg whites until stiff, add a whole 500g box of icing sugar, a bit at a time, then add a squeeze of lemon juice. Use a pallet knife to cover the cake (I'm partial to a spiky snow scene) and leave to set hard.

TOM'S TIPS

If you don't eat it at once, this cake lasts for years. Fill any gaps or crevices in the surface of the cake with marzipan filler. Simnel cake is a traditional Mothering Sunday offering, enjoyed from Lent to Whitsun. It is lush with a slice of Stichelton.

FOOD CHARTER

At Hobbs House, we love making, baking and sharing great food. We cultivate the best of our rich heritage, and we embrace modern thinking and technology. Our deep-rooted values as a company are captured in this Food Charter. Enjoy this age-old ditty that illustrates our hungry values, shaping all that we are, and driving all that we do.

THIS LITTLE PIGGY STAYED AT HOME

Training the next generation

Don't feel sorry for the stay-at-home pig. Hobbs House isn't just a beautiful house on Chipping Sodbury High Street, it's a full-of-life, welcoming, family home that helps us feed our appetite for entertaining. We love to invite people in for a tour of the bakery, or to show off our spectacular wood-fired oven. We get immense pleasure from sharing what we know and do, whether it be for a stint of inspiring work-experience, or a career-changing internship, or (going the whole hog) an apprenticeship in craft baking. For a weaner-sized taster, come on one of our breadmaking courses: everyone leaves with an extra curl in the tail. Screwed to the front of Hobbs House, you'll see our Investors in People plaque, a badge worn with pride, and testimony to our commitment to training future generations in our great and ancient craft. Our foundations go deep, with over 90 years at the oven door, and we've built our home not with straw or sticks, but with bricks.

THIS LITTLE PIGGY WENT TO MARKET

Sourcing the best ingredients

We love to shop, always rooting around for the very best ingredients and hunting for a fair deal. We've learnt where to look, and if it's locally sourced, in season, the best quality and from a trusted producer or supplier, then we can be sure you are getting the real deal. And you'll not pay a penny more than you need to. We've been doing this since 1920; we may be long in the tusk, but we always bring home the bacon.

THIS LITTLE PIGGY HAD ROAST BEEF

We've got a real beef

OK, here comes the squealer: we've got a beef, and I'll tell you why. We really dislike mass-produced 'bread', cheap food that comes at the high cost of making people sick and fat. And that's just for starters. We're squealing and squealing and we want everyone to hear: there is a better way. What we love is true ARTISAN bread, REAL bread, PROPER FOOD. We never rush the process of running our business: when it comes to training, or proving dough, we say, give it time, because it will always be better. Better for you, better for our community and ultimately better for the whole earth. We are overcoming the phoney, plastic-wrapped, pappy bread that proliferates. There's a real bread and food renaissance a-hoof and it's trotting forward with people like you choosing to eat real bread. Help us give bad food the roasting it deserves.

THIS LITTLE PIGGY HAD NONE

Sharing every crumb

Hobbs House has to be sustainable and responsible in everything we do, especially with food waste, which is why we share our surplus with those who don't have enough, giving what we can to FareShare, and encouraging each other to give to the FoodBank. By enjoying food from Hobbs House, you're helping us to muck in and be a force for good in a world that needs it. www.fareshare.org.uk www.trusselltrust.org/foodbank-projects

AND THIS LITTLE PIGGY WENT WEE WEE WEE WEE, ALL THE WAY HOME

Pigs in muck

Picture a helter-skelter. We climb to the top very early in the morning, then try to make every moment of the day enjoyable and empowering (pigs will fly!), by making work at Hobbs House as much fun as is possible in a safe, clean environment. Working every day in high spirits and to an exacting standard transposes itself directly into what we have to offer. By making the whole experience as thrilling as possible, we find it easy to share the exhilaration with anyone who'll let us. I hope you've enjoyed the ride, and we've got you squealing, 'Again, again.' It's troughing good reward for our hard work. Together we can be as content as pigs in muck.

Peace and loaf

INDEX

ACKNOWLEDGEMENTS

Tom

Anna, you are everything to me. A wise, funny, beautiful brick. I couldn't have done this without you.

Thank you, Milo, Beatrix, Josephine and Prudence, for being such lush, brave, smart, hilarious kids, for testing my experiments and being good when I was away.

In-laws Geoff and Sue Keen, for the massive amount of love and support you've given Anna and me over the years. And of course the luscious Lizzie McIntosh.

George Herbert, thank you for so enthusiastically and capably stepping into my role so I could do this.

Henry

First and foremost, thank you to the delectable Jessica Herbert, for holding the fort and feeding the dog.

My awesome in-laws Tony and Anne Hester, thanks for the great support.

Thank you so much to my fantastic team who've held the butchery so well, you make me proud. Jolly Alan with his silly hats and big knives, Paul, Nico, Nathan and Joe.

Together

We'd like to mention, in bent-kneed gratitude:

Our parents, Trev (Babylon) and Polly, you're a wholesome example. Our tremendous sister Clementine for the words. Brothers George (with Zoe), David, Charlie, Archie, Rufus McIntosh and Sam Hester, for being behind the whole project.

Our lovely agent Jess Stone for taking us on, and working so smartly, and all the guys at Independent.

Our inspirational grandparents, David and Margaret Herbert, and John and Marjorie Wells. The faith you've given us is key to who we are, and probably makes us easier to work with.

Big thanks to everyone at Hobbs House, and in particular Alan Wells, Bafana Ncube, Keith Strickland, Jenny Coombe, Carla Moulder, Antony Smith, Sasha Jenner, William Ugle, and especially our uncles and partners at Hobbs House, Clive and Sam Wells, Auntie Ella and Auntie Tory, for your support.

Andrew "digital overlord" Palmer, for creating our cool crest.

Hooray to Sarah Emsley for giving us this awesome opportunity to write the book. Thank you to all the guys at Headline, seriously, great job.

Mari, you really have rolled some illiterate garbage in glitter and made it shine.

Rowan Lawton for her sassy deals.

For making a beautiful book, thanks to all at Smith & Gilmour. Chris Terry, your photographic genius makes the food look better than we could ever have imagined, been a thrill. Signe Johansen and Johanna Kindvall.

Thank you to everyone at Betty, especially Liz and Walter, for having such vision. Neil and Emma for making the cool stuff happen. Director Ben, for squeezing the best out of us. DOP Tom and Steve for great angles. Hannah for building our dream bakery. The all-hearing David, lovely lights Mike and Darren. For help making it happen, Lucy, Harry, Dan and Kat. A huge thank you to our lovely home ec team. Thanks Anna, Emily, Zoe and Beck for being totally on it, wow! Thanks to commissioning editor Katie Horswell, the Features team, Jay Hunt and all at Channel 4 for giving us the green light.